Everyday Ways to Connect with
Your Adopted or Fostered Child

of related interest

The A–Z of Therapeutic Parenting
Strategies and Solutions
Sarah Naish
ISBN 978 1 78592 376 0
eISBN 978 1 78450 732 9

The Strange and Curious Guide to Trauma
Sally Donovan and Emmi Smid
ISBN 978 1 78775 747 9
eISBN 978 1 78775 748 6

**The Seven Core Issues in Adoption and Permanency
Workbook for Children and Teens**
A Trauma-Informed Resource
Allison Davis Maxon
ISBN 978 1 83997 576 9
eISBN 978 1 83997 577 6

Raising Kids with Big, Baffling Behaviors
Brain-Body-Sensory Strategies That Really Work
Robyn Gobbel
Foreword by Bonnie Badenoch
ISBN 978 1 83997 428 1
eISBN 978 1 83997 429 8

Everyday Ways to Connect with Your Adopted or Fostered Child

OVER 200 QUICK AND SIMPLE WAYS TO BUILD RELATIONSHIPS AND OPEN CONVERSATIONS

FIONA BIGGAR

Jessica Kingsley Publishers
London and Philadelphia

First published in Great Britain in 2024 by Jessica Kingsley Publishers
An imprint of John Murray Press

1

A CIP catalogue record for this title is available from the
British Library and the Library of Congress

ISBN 978 1 80501 128 6
eISBN 978 1 80501 129 3

Printed and bound in Great Britain by CPI Group

Jessica Kingsley Publishers' policy is to use papers that are natural,
renewable and recyclable products and made from wood grown in
sustainable forests. The logging and manufacturing processes are expected
to conform to the environmental regulations of the country of origin.

Jessica Kingsley Publishers
Carmelite House
50 Victoria Embankment
London EC4Y 0DZ

www.jkp.com

John Murray Press
Part of Hodder & Stoughton Ltd
An Hachette Company

Contents

Chapter 1

INTRODUCTION

Being a parent is a tough job and parenting a child who has had a challenging start to life is tougher than most. Parenting therapeutically gives our children a chance to recover from the traumas they have experienced by developing new pathways in their brains to help them to reduce their levels of fear and shame, link cause and effect, and understand the world around them. It is a different kind of parenting. We reparent our children to fill in the gaps, we build connections, we strengthen our communication, we use empathy to support our children to recognize and manage their big emotions and we surround them with routine, structure and boundaries to help them feel safe.

Parenting therapeutically does not mean letting our children get away with challenging behaviour, but it does mean that we focus on building the connection in a calm, loving and empathetic way while being clear about the boundaries. It means that we show our child that we accept them as they are and understand that their difficulties stem from their early traumatic experiences. We are the safety net for our children, we give them secure boundaries, at the same time acknowledging that they are frightened, overwhelmed and hurting.

Although we may wish for a magic wand to wave, unfortunately that is not an option. The truth is, we are all doing the best that we can in any given situation, with the choices that we have available in that moment. When it comes to parenting, there is no single right way to do things, no universal truths. All families are different, and all children are unique. You are the expert on your family; no one else knows your children the way that you do. This book will not give you that magic wand, but it will give you more choices. It gives practical and helpful advice from one parent to another in a simple, straightforward way.

This book is aimed at adoptive and foster parents. It should give them lots of practical and easy-to-understand tools and techniques to create a toolbox full of games, language and strategies to use to strengthen the connection with their primary school-age child.

It aims to give adoptive and foster parents an expert there beside them, holding their hand and empowering them to make their life, the life of their child, and the connection between them better. It provides lots of options, lots of small steps, that when taken together make a big difference.

This book is also intended for future adoptive and foster parents, those who are about to begin the most rewarding and challenging journey they will ever experience. It should give them a head start with therapeutic parenting and enable them to plan ahead of time ready for their family expanding.

A little bit about me

I live in Edinburgh with my husband, our two teenage children, two boisterous and affectionate black Labrador dogs and two very chatty cats. Our parenting journey began with the birth of our daughter and continued six years later when our son joined our family at the age of four, through adoption.

Over the years, we have learned so much. We have made lots of mistakes. Given the time again, there are many things I would do differently. However, each year, each new bit of knowledge has put another piece in the jigsaw. We have seen first-hand how seemingly small changes can lead to big shifts in outcome and how each change builds on the last. I cannot know what the future will hold for us, but I know that there will be moments of pure joy and there will be emotionally challenging times and everything in between. That is what family life is like. I know that my journey so far has taught me so much and that I will continue to learn. Being a parent has enriched my life immeasurably, and whatever life bring to us in the future, I know that as a family we have the tools to deal with it together.

I have a psychology degree, and although for much of my professional life I worked in IT in the financial sector, outside work I continued to pursue my passion for helping people by studying counselling, coaching and neuro-linguistic programming, which I used to support my family, friends and colleagues.

Neuro-linguistic programming explores the relationships between how we think (neuro), how we communicate (linguistic) and our patterns of behaviour and emotions (programmes). Over time, it has evolved and grown into a study of human communication and behaviour and has generated lots of practical tools and techniques to assist us all, especially as parents.

Once we became parents for the second time, it was clear that the travel commitments and demands of my finance job would not fit well around family life. I took the big step of becoming self-employed to get the flexibility I needed and utilize the skills I had learned over the years in a professional capacity. I worked as a coach, mentor and trainer with clients and students locally here in Edinburgh, and remotely across the UK.

Alongside this, I worked with Adoption UK, delivering workshops, supporting families through the Buddy programme, and as a volunteer. In 2021, the opportunity arose to join Adoption UK in a permanent role as a parent partner, and until early 2023 I worked, as part of the TESSA programme, one-to-one with adoptive families across Scotland. It is a role that I loved as I am passionate about sharing my knowledge and experience with families to help them, just as others have helped us.

A little bit about this book

In the early years of our adoption journey, I read every book about adoption that was recommended, despite being often exhausted and overwhelmed. I pored over books late at night after the children were asleep. The more I read, the more I learned about the WHY; about the theory of trauma, the impacts on the brain and body and the underlying causes of many behaviours. This was fascinating, and understanding this was helpful, but as a parent who was struggling with challenges every day what I needed most were practical strategies and solutions. I needed to know WHAT to do and HOW to do it. It was as if I was training to be a mechanic when what I needed to learn was how to drive.

This is the book I would have liked to have had in the early years. It contains practical advice in a simple, straightforward way on how to build a more positive, constructive relationship with your child and support them to build resilience and create a more balanced view of themselves and their place in the world. It shows how to enable them (and us) to thrive rather than just survive. It is primarily aimed at children of primary school age, although many of the strategies would also be successful with older children.

Throughout the book there are suggestions of things to try. Some will resonate with you and others may not suit you or your child quite as well. Some may be age appropriate for your child, others may not. Try as many as you can to see which truly fit for your family and then work with the ones that are a great match for you to change your lives for the better. Take your time to reflect and try them a few times with your child. Don't try to do everything at once. Negative patterns are often deeply entrenched, so it will take time and lots of repetition to change them, although you may be surprised how quickly things do change.

Above all, know that you are doing the best you can. Treat yourself with kindness and compassion. Parenting is the most challenging thing that I have ever done. I still mess up and lose control from time to time, I still doubt myself, but I do this much less than I used to. The biggest difference is that now I accept my mistakes, I know that I do not need to be perfect, just good enough, and every day I learn and grow a little bit more as a parent.

A little bit of theory to set the context

Although this book focuses on the *what* and *how*, we need to know a little of the *why* to put our children's behaviour in context – to understand what lies beneath the surface.

Babies rely on those around them to care for them. They are born with innate skills to alert those caregivers to their needs and to keep themselves safe. They cry to get attention, to communicate. Being picked up and comforted provides them with reassurance and safety. At a core level, the baby understands that they are worthy, that they are safe. Over time, this is repeated many times and, even though there may be a delay in a baby's need being met, their overall life experience teaches them that caregivers can be trusted. A baby or child taken into care today will not have this experience. They are likely to have suffered abuse and neglect at the most crucial time in their brain development, from the very person who should have kept them safe.

The legacy of early trauma

Children born into loving, stable homes have an emotional system wired for love, security and seeking attachment. Their needs are met and so their brain builds positive pathways that are *love*-based. Children who are born into a more chaotic and unpredictable environment will build an emotional system wired for fear, insecurity and control. Their needs are not met and they do not feel safe, so their brain builds pathways that are *fear*-based.

For example, a child who is fed regularly develops secure in the knowledge that food is available and will come. This child learns not only what hunger is, but also how that feeling is satisfied. They learn that the world will meet this basic need. A child who is comforted when they cry learns what pain and discomfort feel like and what nurture and comfort feel like too. When a child does not learn this, the world feels unsafe, and the child will struggle to identify hunger or satiety and to differentiate positive and negative feelings and experiences. This leads to dysregulation and an inability to manage the unpredictability of life.

Developmental trauma does not just occur after birth. It occurs from the moment of conception. The birth mother may have been in a state of turmoil and dysregulation before conception and during the pregnancy, leading to high levels of stress hormones such as cortisol and adrenalin. There may have been prenatal drug or alcohol consumption. All these things can pass through the placenta and impact a baby's development in the womb.

The period from conception to the age of three is crucial in how a child's brain develops. It is in these early years that the pathways are laid down. Imagine that the brain is like the map of an unpopulated country. Each thing the child experiences creates connections, creates a track between two points on the map. As experiences repeat, these tracks become more defined. Depending on the level of repetition, some tracks fall into misuse, some stay as minor roads, some become major roads, and those that are used the most become motorways. Routes where there is more repetition become more defined, become easily accessible. Once the child is older, even if their life experiences change and are more positive, there is still this underlying road map. The brain follows the road that is most travelled, and these routes remain as their default.

After a traumatic experience, the human system of self-preservation goes into permanent alert, as if the danger might return at any moment. The brain rushes down the motorways that have been created. Trauma causes a psychological wound – we cannot see it, but it is very real. It is a wound caused by things a child may have perceived as life-threatening: shouting, arguments, abuse, lack of care. There may be lots of different things that have been traumatic for a child, and these experiences have taught them that the world is not a safe place.

It is this legacy of early trauma which makes adopted and fostered children behave in ways that do not seem to make sense or may appear to be an overreaction. Even though they may now be in a safe environment, they cannot unlearn the hardwired responses that are set within their brains. They keep going down the same motorway, repeating their behaviours based on trauma in the past.

Their brain is a bit like a faulty smoke detector that keeps sounding the alert when there is no fire. The alert is triggered not by a fire in the present, but by hardwired reactions to a fire in the past.

Children who have experienced trauma may find it difficult to trust carers, to accept intimacy and allow themselves to be loved. They may seek to sabotage relationships or test them to the point of destruction. They may need to control; they may need constant attention or may find getting attention difficult. They may be overly critical of themselves and of others. They may not have learned what the uncomfortable feelings mean and so are unable to develop self-regulation. They may see the world as frightening and dangerous, and live with a constant fear that they may once again lose everything and everyone they know. The impacts are wide-ranging and complex.

Children who have had early trauma can develop many complex behavioural problems as they grow. This traumatic start will affect every relationship they have; it will colour how they view themselves and the world and how they deal with change or stress. When you are focused on surviving, you do not have the space to be curious and explore, so while a child whose needs have been met will learn and progress, adapting to increasingly complex levels of understanding, the child whose early needs were not met is too busy being scared. Systems wired in a different way will learn differently; what we learn is based on what we expect based on our experience.

Reparenting to fill in the gaps

The child whose needs are met well and frequently grows up feeling loved and nurtured. Their carer is attuned to them and reacts appropriately to their cries. Every time a child's need is met, it is as if we are putting a brick in a wall. We are building a solid, well-constructed and robust structure, a wall that is cemented together with love and nurture and is strong enough to withstand storms and adversity.

Sadly, where a child does not have their needs met, their internal wall has bricks missing, and those bricks that are there may be badly placed without support and without the cement that love and nurture would have added. Traumatized children will have the double misfortune of missing the 'normal' development input alongside the impacts of early life trauma. Their internal wall will be unstable and be prone to crumble or collapse under pressure. Unfortunately, this deficit cannot be seen from the outside, so it is often overlooked. It is only when we look closely through our trauma-informed lens that we can see the damage inside.

To survive, there are several fundamental needs in life. At the most basic level we need to have our physical requirements met. We need to breathe, we need food, water, warmth and sleep to stay alive. We need shelter and clothing. We need to feel safe and secure. Only where these fundamental needs are met will we be able to seek to meet higher level needs such as love, acceptance, belonging and a positive sense of self.

Imagine if you were shipwrecked on a deserted island, where there are limited resources and many predators. What would your mind be focused on? Would you be able to think about anything except food, water, shelter and safety? Every waking moment would be consumed by ensuring that your basic needs are met. You would be on constant high alert, ready to run to escape from wild animals. There would be no space to think about big questions in life or to develop new skills. All your mental resources would be focused on survival, and it would be an incredibly stressful and exhausting way to live.

A child who experiences early life trauma develops in an environment like that deserted island. They have not had their fundamental needs met. Their brain has developed with its focus on food, water, warmth and safety, removing the capacity to develop other things. Their brain has a deeply rooted view of the world as somewhere fundamentally unsafe where everything is unpredictable. There is a belief that all of this will be erased when a child is put in a nice new home with caring, consistent, loving adults. However, moving a child to an environment where their needs are met will not be enough by itself for the child to feel and believe they are safe. When a child sees the world as dangerous and unreliable then they can never be sure of what might happen next, and the possibilities are terrifying. Their brain is still living on that deserted island, fearful for its safety. It will take time, and lots of repetition, to rewire these patterns in their brain and enable them to fulfill more than just their basic needs.

Parenting a child who is hurting

Becoming a parent is one of the biggest learning curves we will ever encounter. As adoptive or foster parents, we have the added complexity that our children come to us having started their life elsewhere, with the associated life experience. Adoption and fostering create the supportive family environment that children need to thrive, although while adoption and fostering are a positive new beginning, they do not take away the negative early experiences that adopted and fostered children will have faced and, sadly, the act of being adopted or fostered itself brings trauma and loss. Every adopted or fostered child will have suffered the loss of their birth family and possibly of one or more foster families. It is a sad reality that more than 80 per cent of children who come into the care system will have experienced abuse, trauma or neglect early in their lives, and the impacts of trauma, drugs or alcohol in pregnancy may also have had damaging effects.

Adoption and fostering can be, and usually are, transformative experiences for children. Loving and committed adoptive and foster parents can make an enormous difference. We can provide the nurture and consistency that was missing in their early years. Repair can happen, but it takes time and requires lots of repetition and consistent and nurturing care. For adoptive and foster parents, this can sometimes feel relentless. Giving this care can be challenging in the face of an angry, rejecting child whose fear and insecurity are at times hard to manage.

As adoptive and foster parents, we need to remember that our children's behaviour is their way of communicating. Our children may not be able to recognize or understand their fears and emotions – and these 'big feelings' can come out as challenging behaviours. We cannot erase their past experiences, but we can help them to deal with them and to build new, more resourceful behaviours by practising therapeutic reparenting.

Parenting children who have experienced trauma can shake our core beliefs and can push our buttons in ways that we could never have imagined when we started our journey into adoption or fostering. It can be soul-destroying to put so much care and attention into building a relationship with a child who appears disengaged, distant or even hostile. Alongside this, our support network may prove less help than we had hoped, as often friends and family do not understand, or may offer well-meaning advice on using traditional parenting methods. We may face criticism that we are being too soft, or that our children need discipline. It can be hard to stick to our guns and parent therapeutically when faced with the judgement and lack of understanding of others around us.

When we consider how we parent our children, it can also be helpful to reflect on our own upbringing – we may parent just how we were parented, or in an opposite way as a reaction to our own experiences. We may have red lines that we do not realize are there, and voices in our heads reinforcing patterns from our past. The world around us can reinforce traditional parenting methods that can undermine our best intentions to do things differently. We may also need to reflect on how our children were parented in the past both with birth families and foster carers.

We must learn what we need to let go. It is not about what is right or what is wrong, it is about learning what works for our children. It is about changing our perspective, changing how we deal with things, recognizing that some of the things we are doing are not working, letting these go and trying something else. If what we are doing is not working, then we are not losing anything. It is not about changing the child, but about changing their view of us and their world, which will lead in time to changes in behaviour.

Always remember that you are doing the best you can. There will be times when you feel you have smashed it, times when you feel you could have done better and there will be moments when you feel you have failed catastrophically. Nobody always gets it right. This is normal – parenting is hard and parenting children who have suffered trauma is doubly difficult. Good enough really is good enough, and although being an adoptive or foster parent is challenging at times, it is also hugely rewarding, and your efforts are transforming the life of your child.

Chapter 2

BUILDING CONNECTIONS

The connections we make to each other are the invisible threads that hold us together. They build our feeling of belonging as a family and a sense of shared experience and a shared future.

The human brain is under constant development. Every interaction we have with the world builds connections in our brains. The connections that we make are shaped by our life experiences. Although the brain continues to develop into adulthood, the early years are critical, as at this stage every experience is a new one and many more connections are laid down than are generated at any other age. At this stage of development, a baby is taking the knowledge they get from their environment and building their view of the world.

Crying is the only way a baby can communicate their needs. A small baby does not know what they want or need, they just know something is wrong. They cannot identify that feeling as hunger, as a dirty nappy, or as being tired. When a baby cries, a good enough carer tries different things to help the child, such as offering milk, a nappy change or a cuddle. They try different responses to see what meets the need of the baby, and in time, both they and the baby learn to differentiate different needs and meet them. Babies learn what they need from the responses they get. Through their needs being met by the caregiver, trust develops, the baby feels safe and learns what the internal feelings mean. In time, the child can work out how to meet those needs for themselves. They learn how to self-regulate. When a baby's needs are met, they learn that the world is a safe place, that they are lovable and wanted and that their caregivers can be trusted. When a child's needs are met, they learn about themselves, about their needs and how to view themselves. The child builds an internal model of self, based on how the outside world reacts to them. We learn who we are through how others interact with us.

Children who have experienced inconsistent care may not give clear cues on what their needs are. They may not even know themselves what their needs are. Babies who did not get their needs met in this way may never have learned to identify their internal feelings and so may not know that they are hungry, frightened or hurt. This means that they may not cry when they are hurt, they may not ask for food when they are hungry. This can make it difficult for us as parents to read what is going on for them. Where a baby has poor or inconsistent care, they learn to mistrust caregivers and perceive the world as a hostile place. They learn that the only person that they can rely on is themselves. They develop little sense of self-worth and view themselves as unworthy of love. They exist in a world where they do not feel safe.

Early experience of caregivers creates a child's expectations of how emotionally reliable and trustworthy other people are. This shapes how comfortable (or uncomfortable) they are in relationships and how they feel about giving or receiving love. To maintain a healthy relationship with another person, we need to be able to manage connection and disconnection. When a loved one leaves, we need to be able to disconnect and feel comfortable that they will continue to exist and that they will return. When they return, we need to be able to reconnect. People who have secure attachments can maintain these connections and reconnections, but a child who experienced early life trauma is likely to have developed insecure attachment and will tend to struggle with balancing these. They may manage to connect or to disconnect but may have difficulty in managing both. The single most important factor for children in developing relationships is having at least one stable and committed bond with a supportive parent, caregiver or other adult. These relationships provide the scaffolding and protection to buffer children from the effects of developmental disruption.

Whatever a child's history, child-centred, connected parenting is key to a secure, loving relationship. The keys to forming a healthy attachment are the same whether a child has been adopted, fostered or born into our family. When a child comes to us with a history, we may worry whether they will have the capacity to form an attachment to us, and whether we will form an attachment to them. One wonderful moment of love and connection does not make an attachment between parent and child, and neither does one difficult moment mean an attachment problem. A feeling of connectedness may come quickly, or it may take more time. In some moments, the connection will feel secure, in others less so. Attachment evolves and changes.

Having a strong, reliable parental presence builds the connection. We want to be their physical and psychological safe place – their safe harbour, sheltering them within our walls, keeping the water around them calm even when it is choppy outside. The more we connect, the more our children feel safe, loved and worthy of that love.

A sense of belonging

Feeling connected to others is central to our children's self-esteem. Adopted and fostered children can feel a sense of disconnection, of being other, and so the more we can reinforce the connection, the sense of belonging, the better they will feel about themselves and their place in the world.

One of the greatest ways to build a sense of belonging in your child is to spend time with them. Giving someone your undivided attention reinforces the idea that they are worthy of love, that they are special, that they are the centre of your world...and what is not to like about that!

As parents, we know instinctively that our children need to spend quality time with us; however, for most of us, time is something we do not have. So how can we find time when we feel we do not have any to spare? Here are few ideas of how to fit things into even the busiest lives.

Encouraging conversation

Ask about their interests: Show them that you are interested in what they like and that you want to be part of their life. Ask interested questions. Build little connections. Establish links. Show them over and over that you are there for them. Reinforce that you are their safe harbour. When we show interest, we build confidence in ourselves and our child. It makes everyone feel good. Sometimes we may have to feign interest, as our children's favourite things may not spark our interest, but always remember how good it feels when someone is interested in us.

It is good to talk: There are quite often small slots in the day, when driving, waiting for an appointment, on the bus or in a café, where the unused time could be utilized to connect with your child. Here are a few conversation starters to use to prompt more fruitful discussions. Think about your response to the question before you ask your child, as it helps if you can join in with your version and share the discussion:

- Tell me three things you are good at.
- What new skill have you learned recently?
- What do your friends like about you? And what do you like about them?
- Can you think of a special memory?
- If you had a superpower, what would it be and why?
- If you were invisible, where would you go and what would you do?
- If we could go anywhere for a day, where would you want to go?
- If you could change one thing about me, what would it be?
- If you could be anyone else, who would you be and why?
- What are the three most interesting things about you?
- What is your favourite book? What do you like about it? Do you have a favourite character?
- When do you feel most proud of who you are?

Chatting about themselves helps our children to feel that we are interested and to see themselves in a positive way.

One-to-one time: Organize a slot where you can be one-to-one with your child. Try to find a slot at least once a month, and ideally mark the slots on the calendar so that your child can see that you are giving them priority. If there are siblings, organize for them to be with their other parent or at a friend's or relative's house. It does not have to be for a prolonged period; what matters is that your child gets your undivided attention for that slot.

Do something you both love: Teach your child how to do something you love, such as cooking, gardening, fishing, a favourite sport. Enjoy doing it together and perhaps in time your passion will become theirs and will be something you can bond over for life.

Head in the clouds: Work with your child to create a word cloud filled with their qualities. Spend time together agreeing all the positive words that you want to include. Think about your child's qualities, activities they enjoy, what they want to be, adjectives that describe them, their physical attributes. There are various free online applications to use that let you plug in text and they produce the word cloud for you, so it is a lot easier than it may at first appear. Just search online for 'word cloud' and you will see lots of different options to choose from.

Fun activities to do together

Random acts of kindness: Surprising our children with a random act of kindness can be a lovely way to build connections too. Do something small, something simple, something that makes them feel good. Make their favourite tea or go to a park that they love to visit. It reinforces their positive self-image. It's about them. Make sure it's about what they would want. Show them that you know them, that you understand what they like and that you want them to enjoy themselves.

Enlist their help: Children love to help. Does the carpet need to be vacuumed? Let them do it with you. Does the recycling need to be sorted? Does the table need to be set for dinner? Do it together. Need to make dinner? Let them help with the preparation process. While it might be messier and it may take longer in the beginning, you are teaching them essential life skills and in time your children will become your greatest helpers and they will look back and remember these as special times with you.

Let your child take the lead: Children with positive interactions at the start of their lives have a central belief that they are at the centre of the universe. This is an important part of their development and helps to support a positive sense of self and future independence. Our children may not have experienced this, so create opportunities for your child to be in the centre, to be in charge. Play *Follow the Leader* or *Simon Says*; give them control of what happens next in a contained way.

Measuring: Measure your child's height, length of arms, feet, hands and so forth. Keep a record for later comparisons. Measure surprising things, such as their smile, how high they can jump, their hug. Keep a record so they can see how much they have grown. Or peel an apple or use sugar laces to measure with that so they can eat their smile, their height or even their foot!

Build a den: Use sofa cushions, chairs and blankets to build a den. Have fun in the den, read stories by torchlight, play games and even eat in there.

Make a cardboard fort or castle: Use cardboard boxes from the recycling to build a fort, or a castle, or any structure that fits with your child's interests. Have fun decorating it. Colour it in, stick things on it. Go wild!

Make a recycling model: Use cardboard and plastic from the recycling to build a monster, a robot, a dinosaur, a car, a rocket – anything that sparks your child's imagination.

Make an ice tower: Use a large, straight plastic bottle with a wide neck. Put toys and other waterproof items inside and fill it with water. Put it in the freezer until it is frozen solid. Cut the bottle off and then with your child try different ways to melt the ice and release the toys. Use salt, cold water, hot water, experiment together.

Indoor bowling: Use rolled up socks or a soft ball and empty cans or plastic bottles to create a homemade indoor bowling alley.

Basketball sock toss: Use wastepaper bins or laundry baskets to create different targets. Use rolled up socks or a soft ball to toss into the targets. Take turns to see how many you can get in the baskets. To make it more complex for older children, make some targets smaller or further away and award different points for each, depending on the level of difficulty. You can even make it a competition to see who can get the highest score in a minute.

Cotton wool blow football: Lie on the floor on your tummies and blow cotton wool balls back and forth trying to get the cotton ball past each other or both blowing at the same time to keep the ball in the middle.

Home car wash: Get together toy cars, trucks and rockets and line them up in the bath for a mini car wash. Dunk them in soapy water and wash it off with water squirters or a shower spray.

Disco inferno: Dim the lights, close the curtains, have a torch each and sing and dance along to some fun tracks.

Fifteen minutes of fun: Work out a few activities together that can be done in 15 minutes and agree to do one of the activities of your child's choosing each day. Create a physical list on paper that can be put up somewhere prominent so that they can look at it to make their choice. We had a pictorial chart of all the activities, but if your child is a good reader, you could just list them. Even when you are terribly busy it feels manageable to agree to take 15 minutes out. You might not think that it is a significant amount of time, but it is not the length of time that matters, but the quality of it, and for that time your child is getting your undivided attention. If you are short of time and keeping to the 15 minutes is important, use a 15-minute sand timer so your child can see the passing of time and knows when the activity is coming to an end, which will ease the transition.

Fun connection-building activities for the whole family

Scavenger hunts: These are a wonderful way to get everyone involved and can be done indoors or outside. Create a list of things for them to find. Perhaps have a theme such as nature or colours or the senses. Or you can hide things for them to find.

Treasure hunts: Like a scavenger hunt, but instead of hunting for lots of items they are working towards finding one final treasure. You can do this with a series of clues leading on to the next and finally to the treasure. Or use letters for them to find, which they can rearrange to make the name of the place where they will find the treasure. If you are doing this with multiple children, engineer it so that they will not be in competition. For example, if they are hunting tokens for Easter eggs, make each child a specific colour, or if there are letters to find, make a separate set for each child.

Hand and footprints: Using paint and a large sheet of paper make handprints and footprints of all the family. You can even do bottom prints for maximum hilarity. The resulting artwork will be a lovely reminder of a fun family day.

Creating the storm: Cycle through these actions so that together you create a storm. Start with rubbing your hands together for wind, then move to patting thighs for a rain shower, building into clapping hands for heavy rain, and moving up to stomping feet with clapping hands for thunder, making as much noise as you all can, and then calming back down through rain to just wind again. This is a fantastic way to get rid of pent-up energy and create a positive mood.

Blow over: All sit down in a circle and take turns to blow each other over. Make the falling overs very silly and exaggerated so you all have a laugh. Encourage your children to take bigger longer breaths in through their nose and puff out hard. This encourages deep breathing, which is helpful for regulation.

Mirroring: Stand facing everyone else and move your arms, legs and any part of your body or face. Everyone else copies you. Do it fast, slow, in a rhythm. Play about with it, have fun together.

Traffic lights: Ask everyone to do something physical such as running, walking, star jumps, hopping, dancing, sitting. Say green light to start, red light to stop.

Special handshake: Make up a special handshake together, taking turns to add new moves such as a high five, finger wiggles, bottom bumps and so on. You can build the moves up over time and make it into a family ritual.

Build an indoor obstacle course: Create an obstacle course indoors using chairs, cushions, blankets or anything you have to hand. Get your child included in the choices and the building. Make things that you need to go over or under, or even add clothes or items that you must put on as you go. Perhaps put on multiple hats – the sillier the things you add, the funnier it can be.

Build an outdoor obstacle course: Create an obstacle course outdoors. Work together to make things to go around, under or jump over. Add beams or lines to balance on. Set things up to weave between. If you have a dog, see if the dog can do it with you. Or even create your own doggy agility course. You can go round the course together with your child or go round separately, whatever works for the age and stage of your child.

Follow the leader: Take turns to be the leader, and everyone else follows and copies the leader. As the leader, you can do silly walks, dances, jumps – anything that you can all do and that the space allows.

Family band: Using boxes and bottles from the recycling, make home-made musical instruments. Add elastic band to make strings. Play them together as a family band. Maximum noise and fun!

When we spend quality time with our children, we reinforce that they matter, that we love them. It says how important they are to us. When we do things together as a family it builds a sense of belonging and together-ness. A sense of family builds everyone's self-esteem.

Checking in

During the day, commentate in a positive way with your child. Show your child that they are in your thoughts and that you love them. Reinforce how much you care. For example, say, 'Good morning, how did you sleep? I hope you had a good night. I missed you while you were sleeping' or, 'You look very smart in that top. The colour makes your eyes sparkle' or, 'Toast – good choice'. Perhaps count their fingers and toes, or their freckles. Check that they still have the same button nose, or curly hair. Notice lots of special things about your child that reassure them that everything is still the same and that you and they remain connected. In these interactions, you are building a positive sense of themselves, helping them to see that they are loved and worthy of that love. As a wonderful way to highlight how far they have come, talk about how they can do something today that they could not do last week or last month, and thereby build their self-belief and sense of achievement.

Let your child know that even when you are not with them physically, they are in your thoughts. Write notes and drop them into their lunch boxes. Or leave a post-it note on their bedside table or in the fridge on their favourite yogurt. Or laminate a photo of the two of you together having fun and put it in their school jacket pocket or hang it on their bag. Be creative!

Tell your children that you love them. Say it often and for no reason other than to show that they are special to you. That they belong in your heart.

Your child may fear that if they do something wrong or disappoint you, you will no longer love them. Use language that stresses that you love them unconditionally, that you love them even if you are in a bad mood or they have misbehaved. It is the behaviour that you do not like, the child is still loved. Separate the behaviour from the child. For example, say, 'I love you, I just don't like it when you...'

If you do get cross, then own it. Tell them that you are sorry, model taking responsibility and let them see that you are human too. Have a conversation later when you are both calm and able to reflect. Mistakes will happen; we are all doing the best we can in any given moment and talking about it helps your child to learn and repairs and strengthens the relationship.

Periodically, check in with them. It does not have to be prolonged; a fleeting connection is okay. This can be an effective counterbalance when things may have been challenging earlier in the day. By checking in you are repairing the relationship, rebuilding the connection and reminding your child that they are loved unconditionally.

Parent the inner child

Although our children's early life experiences will have impacted on their brain development, they still have the capacity to make good progress. There will be some things that they cannot do that others of their chronological age can handle with ease, and other things they do that are beyond their years. Their ability to cope will go up and down; what they can manage one day they may not be able to handle the next. It's important to think not of their age, but of the stage they are at and to meet them in a stage-appropriate way, not an age-appropriate way. Their developmental age may be different in different areas of their life. For example, an 11-year-old child could be operating at around age 11 for living skills but could be around nine for language and expression, and closer to seven in their social skills.

We need to work with them to rewire their brains from the bottom up. This approach is not quick, it is an intensive and protracted process. Each tiny step builds on the last. It is a bit like throwing stones into a lake – for ages there will be nothing to see, but under the surface the pile is building until eventually it will break the surface.

Children who have suffered trauma need help to build connections with caregivers and create the attachments that were missing in their early years. Therapeutic parenting meets the child's unmet needs at their pace and level. Many of the behaviours that we observe in our children are ones that would have been viewed very differently in a younger child. For example, if an eight-year-old denies taking a biscuit from the tin it gets classed as lying. If a three-year-old does the same, we find it endearing, even if they are surrounded by evidence and clearly did eat that biscuit!

Children who have experienced persistent trauma will not be consistently operating at their chronological age. They are likely to often be operating at a much younger level. Inside that eight-year-old is a toddler covered in crumbs! When there is a difference between what a child can achieve developmentally and what the world expects of them, that can take a toll on the child. When we meet them at the age they are operating at, and parent them in a way matched to that, then we support them to meet their need. We go back with them in order to go forwards. Developmental reparenting teaches us as parents to move from focusing on the behaviour to wondering what the unmet need is and what they are trying to communicate. When we as parents, teachers and other carers adapt our expectations and our attitude, see the child's behaviour as communication and accept that it comes from a place of fear and a feeling of lack of safety, we see their actions in a different way, and our responses become different too.

A child who experienced early life trauma and loss will have missed many stages of development. Help them to experience things that they may have missed. Help your child to be seen and heard and have their feelings acknowledged. Draw them out and build confidence to strengthen the connection. Play with them in ways that a younger child might enjoy, games like *Peek-a-Boo*, *This Little Piggy* or nursery rhymes. Watch TV programmes or read books that a younger child might enjoy. Singing and dancing is also good for the spirits. The rhythm in songs and music can help everyone regulate their emotions and be very playful. It is about creating a playful and caring child-to-adult interaction. Help them to play in the way their younger self could not and let them move on in their own time. Here are a few ideas of games that are fun to play together:

Beep and honk: Press the child's nose and say 'beep', then press their chin and say 'honk!' Guide your child to do it back. Make different noises for different parts of the body and get them to make ones up too.

Cotton wool ball or feather touches: Touch different places with a cotton wool ball or a feather and get them to guess where you are touching. Let them do it to you too. This is a great game for building regulation, as the child is learning to manage their anticipation.

Pop cheeks: Inflate your cheeks with air and help your child to pop them with their hands. You can do it to them too.

Bubbles: Put some washing up liquid on a plate with a little water. Using a straw, blow into the liquid to make bubbles.

Sorting shapes and colours: Use Lego, Duplo or any other multicoloured or multi-shaped items. Work with your child to sort them into bowls by colour or by shape.

Adapt a song or nursery rhyme: Sing a familiar song but add your child's name into the words. For songs like 'You Are My Sunshine', sing 'my [child's name] sunshine', or with 'Row Your Boat', sing '[child's name] is such a dream' at the end.

The legacy that early trauma leaves with a child means that as adoptive and foster parents we need not only to parent our children but to reparent them to fill in the gaps and make up for the early life gaps in learning and the negative brain pathways that will have become embedded. We learn to parent a traumatized child in a therapeutic, connective way that is calm and without confrontation and supports them at their own pace as they catch up emotionally, socially and academically. It takes time to get to grips with where our children are and what works. Pre-birth and post-birth trauma create layers of difficulty and therapeutic parenting helps us peel back the layers.

Out of sight, out of mind

Understanding about object constancy is something most children develop as they grow. It is rooted in attachment. With a secure attachment, when a parent leaves the room, the child understands that they still exist and is comforted by that. Children who did not build early secure attachments will not have developed this object constancy. Instead, they will have an 'out of sight, out of mind' view of the world. If someone is not in sight, they cease to exist for the child. This breeds fear and uncertainty.

Building object constancy in our children takes lots of repetition. Start by deliberately leaving the room briefly and returning, to help your child to see that even though you leave, you come back. Build up the length of your absence if they are comfortable with that. Play games like hide-and-seek or have a treasure hunt, where they return to you with each thing they find, around the house or garden. These are great fun for everyone and modelling going away and coming back is a powerful way to teach our children how to handle this feeling of loss and fear in an incremental way.

If they are going to be away from you for a longer time, leave them notes or items to find. Perhaps use a transitional object like a picture of the family, or something of yours for them to keep for you. For an older child with a phone, send text messages to show that you are thinking of them. When you see them, talk about how you thought about them, perhaps bring them something small, a snack, a toy or a photo you took on your phone that they would like – anything that shows that they were in your thoughts even though you were not with them.

Behave as if they have reacted in the way you expect

If your child rejects your advances, if they turn away, pretend that they looked pleased and opened their arms. Model the behaviour that you want to see. Look right at them, smile, open your arms, and say welcoming words about how you missed them. Their behaviours are not aimed at you. Remember, it is likely that they are rejecting you because they are terrified that you will reject them and this is their only way to have any control.

It is easy to feel hurt when a child pushes you away or says something that feels hurtful. The child does not seek to reject you, these are expressions of difficult feelings for them – expressions of fear, frustration and anger. Acknowledge their feeling, give it a name. Let them see that it is okay to feel bad sometimes.

Remembering the good times

When we are rushing about busy with our daily treadmill of work and school, it can be easy to lose sight of the fact that we are a family. It is fun from time to time to focus on activities that make us stop and take stock of ourselves and the rest of the family and what we mean to each other. These activities also have the added benefit of making us parents feel good about ourselves too!

Surround them with memories: Take photos of you all having fun and display the photos in the house. Make sure to put one or two where the child can see them from their bed as a reminder that they belong and they are loved. Make handprint and footprint paintings, make pottery, crafts, anything that has a product that can be displayed at home. Display their artwork in a prominent place. Surround them with good memories and a positive sense of their place in the world.

That was the day we: Make up a photo album of fun times, which they can look at in their room. Talk through the photos often with them. It can be a lovely bedtime activity. Reminisce about family days and how much you enjoyed them. Talk through events that happened and strengthen their memory and positive sense of themselves and their place within the family. What do you remember? What do they remember? What did they do? What did you like about what they did? How did it make you feel towards them? Talking about happy memories brings back the emotions of the day and brings us closer together. Shared experiences bring us together and generate a sense of belonging. Shared positive history makes us feel good about ourselves and each other.

A trip down memory lane: Get out photo albums or videos of you when you were a child. Look through the pictures and talk to your child about the memories that they evoke. How old were you in the picture? What do you remember about being a child? What were your parents like with you? Where are you? Who are the other people there? Talking to your children about your childhood helps them to see you as a person, not just as a parent. It also helps them to share the experience of growing up with you and can be a wonderful opening to conversations about things that they are experiencing.

Choose a person of the week: Each week, pick a member of the family to be the person of the week. Once a day (just after teatime worked well for us), the other family members need to think of something good that person did that day, or just something nice about them, and write it on a combined sheet. Put the sheet up somewhere where everyone can see it.

At the end of the week, discuss the positive comments with the person of the week, and choose next week's person. Give the person of the week their completed sheet to keep.

A box of delights: This is a similar exercise to the person of the week, it just does it in a slightly different way and compliments the whole family at once. This can be helpful for children who find it challenging when the focus is on another person (or on them). Once a day, each family member takes one piece of paper for each of the other family members and writes a sentence about something good that person did that day, or just something nice about them. They need to write the person's name on the paper too. Once you have finished, put all the positive notes into a box. At the end of the week, pass them all out so everyone can enjoy the positive comments about them from other family members. Talk together about what you each said about each other.

Strengthening family ties with tradition

Every family has things they do that are special to them – the quirks that may have been part of the family for generations or that started one day and became something you do. When we have something that we do together that is just ours, it gives a powerful sense of belonging, of being part of a special club. They can be big or small. Whatever size they are, they cement your togetherness as a family.

They can be things that happen regularly, like having a takeaway on the first Saturday of the month, or Movie Fridays or things that happen only on a particular day. For example, in our family we have a treasure hunt on Christmas Day, with the treasure being one of their Christmas presents. They each have individual clues to locations around the house and garden where they find letters that they need to unscramble to identify the location of their gift. It started as a way to burn energy and entertain them on Christmas morning when the kids were young, but as teenagers they still love their treasure hunt. Having these traditions creates structure and belonging.

Some traditions within a family will be ones that no one outside the family understands – the little rituals and in-jokes of your family club. They could be things like silly names for objects or people, or a special wave, or something you always do or say when you say goodbye, or made-up songs or dances. It could be something you always do at a particular time, such as a dance to a theme song, or a phrase you all use – anything that builds that sense of sharing, of belonging. I like to embarrass my kids by doing strange dances to selected TV theme tunes. It started as a bit of fun to help them relax but has grown into an expected introduction to some TV watching. They loudly object every time, but it creates a thread back through all the other times I did it, and it builds connection. These rituals help our children feel that there is normality in times of change or when they are somewhere new. For example, when you are away overnight, sticking to the sameness of the bedtime routine and the things you do together will create a sense of familiarity even though the surroundings are unfamiliar.

Think about where you can introduce traditions into your family. Create regular slots where you do things together or have some silly things you do or say that are special to you. On special days, like birthdays or the last day of school, have things you do together to mark them. Create rituals around decorating the tree or Christmas Day itself. These traditions glue us together as families. They create a sense of security and belonging for our children and build shared experiences that have special meaning for us all.

Meeting their needs when you are busy

In family life, there are frequently times when we feel like we are being pulled in multiple directions. I know I sometimes feel as if I am stretched tissue thin and am ready to break apart. When we are trying to make tea, or work, or have a conversation, and our child is asking endless questions or wanting to play a game it can feel overwhelming and we can feel irritated by it.

When children behave like this it is often described as 'attention-seeking behaviour' and in a way it is. They do want our attention. However, this phrase has developed an extremely negative connotation, a sense that the child is trying to manipulate the adults, and that this behaviour is bad. Well-meaning friends and family members may offer advice to ignore the child because if you give in to them you are just encouraging the behaviour.

Young children can struggle to understand that they are valued when they are not getting attention from the other person. They see their value as reflected in how the other person interacts with them. Children who have had inconsistent care are likely to find this especially challenging. When we recognize that their behaviour is not attention seeking but instead is connection seeking, then we can deal with it in an appropriate way and help them to develop a healthier view that they are valued all the time, not just when we are paying attention to them.

Maintaining connection without giving constant attention

In the early part of this chapter there are lots of ideas to build the connection, and when we work on these then our child's attention cup will be getting topped up regularly so the need for connection will be reduced. However, regardless of how often we top up that attention cup, there will still be times when our child seeks connection and we cannot be available at that precise moment for them. In these moments, there are things we can do to get us the space we require while still showing them that they matter to us.

Forward planning is essential so that you are prepared when the moment arises. Think about some tasks that your child enjoys and can do unaided. Resist the temptation to add chores in. This is supposed to be fun. Pick tasks that would take them around 15 minutes, as that is probably as long as they will feel comfortable being self-directed. Choose inside and outside tasks, ensuring that all are safe for them to do alone. Work on them with your child so they make suggestions and are invested in the choices. Make sure they know it is about them having fun, that sometimes you are busy, but you still love them even when you are doing something else.

Here are a few examples to get you thinking:

- practise keepy-uppy in the garden
- play with lego
- read a story
- draw a picture
- colour in a picture
- practise shooting goals between two cones
- make a paper chain
- skip
- do a jigsaw
- make up a dance
- throw balls in the garden for the dogs.

Once you have the list, put it somewhere that your child can see so you can direct them to it. How you display the tasks depends on what works for you and for your child. We had a pictorial chart of all the activities, but if your child is a good reader, you could write them as a list, or write them on lolly sticks and put them in a jar.

Ideally, put a 15-minute sand timer with the list so your child can see the passing of time. It can also be helpful to gather some of the things together by the list – for example, a story book, paper, pencils, a colouring book – so they do not have to go looking for what they need.

The next time your child seeks connection when you are busy, you have an option to redirect them, to get a 15-minute delay so you can finish what you are doing without interruption. When it does happen, make sure your child knows that it is just for 15 minutes, that you love them and that you will be there for them after the 15 minutes. For example, 'I must answer some emails for work just now. I love doing things with you, but if I do not get these finished then I will not have the things I need for my meeting tomorrow. If you go and have fun doing one of your 15-minute tasks, by the time you get back I will have finished my work and we can chop up the vegetables for tea together. I love doing that with you, you are a great chopper!' When they return, make that connection, give them the one-to-one attention they need and thank them for giving you that time to get things done. The more you do this, the more they will realize that they can do things themselves and that you still love them even when you are not together. In time, the length of time that they can be away from you will increase.

Making a physical connection

With babies and tiny children, the opportunities for physical closeness occur naturally. With older children, this can take more effort to engineer. Look for opportunities throughout the day to give them a hug, ruffle their hair or touch their shoulder. Do anything that makes a physical connection, but keep it to things that you know they are comfortable with and welcome. When you are watching TV or reading a book, cuddle up, snuggle under a blanket to share body warmth and feel connected. Physical connections reinforce the emotional connections with the release of oxytocin, which is often called the happiness or love hormone, creating a feeling of well-being and strengthening the bond between parent and child.

Positive touch also leads to the release of serotonin, which calms the mind and body, and dopamine, which regulates attention and helps with sleep. Massage is a lovely way to create that connection. It can be done on bare skin or through clothes and with firm or light pressure. It can be on the body or on hands or feet or on the head. There are lots of ways to do this and it is a wonderful way to build closeness. Always check in with your child that they are comfortable and enjoying the experience. Starting a dialogue with a child so that they know it is okay to say that they do not want to be touched is a good life lesson.

Many kids love the feeling of massage on bare skin, and it has a soothing effect, especially at bedtime. You do not have to use any creams or oils but if you would like to, then it is lovely to have more than one scent to choose from as kids love choosing and it gets them more involved. If your child is happy to use an oil but finds scent difficult, use a plain oil like a vegetable oil. Try to keep contact throughout, only removing one hand once the other hand is touching them. Use firm, even pressure rather than light tickly fingers. Keep your movements relaxed and rhythmic. If your child particularly enjoys massage, you can go the whole hog and have a 'spa day' with a long soaking bubble bath followed by lying on towels on a table or bed, with soft music and scented candles flickering while they have a massage. A real treat!

You can do a head massage too, massaging under the hair with your finger, lightly pulling the skin up, pressing fingers and thumb towards each other, rubbing the temples and round the hairline. Some children will enjoy lots of pressure, others less. Keep checking in with them to see what they like.

If your child is unsure of a head or body massage, how about trying a foot or hand massage? There are loads of inexpensive hand and foot creams on the market to experiment with, to see which scent and feel your child likes. It is simple and effective – just rub the cream in using different pressures and varying lengths of stroke, including some long strokes going up the arm or leg.

For some children, even hand or foot contact can be too much. Touch can be scary for children with experience of abuse or neglect so all the following techniques can be done over clothes which can feel less intrusive. They can be done anytime, anywhere without the need for any additional equipment. Be led by your child, take things at their pace.

Fun massage strokes

Do what feels comfortable and tailor the pressure to suit your child. Some children will love heavy pressure, others will only tolerate a light touch. Use even pressure so it isn't tickly and keep contact with the skin, only removing a hand once the other hand has made contact.

Straight pushing: Push your thumb or finger in a straight line.

Arcs: Starting with your thumbs at a single location, push them apart in two arcs.

Kneading/the claw: With fingers outstretched, lightly pull the skin up (a bit like the claw that picks up toys in a fairground – or in *Toy Story*!).

Small circle pushing: Use your thumb, two fingers or the palm of your hand to make a circle with gentle but firm pressure.

Karate chops: Do quick chops using the edge of your hands, alternating hands rapidly.

Spider fingers: Make rapid tapping finger movements, with both hands darting about like the legs of a spider.

Shoulder squeezes: With hands on their shoulders standing either in front or behind them, press fingers and thumbs towards each other compressing and squeezing up at the same time.

You can make these into a game or get the child to do them on you or their siblings. There are great opportunities for different types of touch and different pressures, and lots of bonding too.

Fun massage games – for young children

Follow a favourite story: Make the movement of the characters or the action on their back. Make sure it is a story that you both know well. Stories that work well have lots of repetition and rhythm and suggest clear actions that you can do. 'Going on a Bear Hunt' works brilliantly for this, with the wavy swishy swashy grass, the splash splosh river, and the repetition of going over and under and through, not to mention the headlong dash back home! 'The Gruffalo' is good too, as it has lots of characters who all move in quite different ways.

The animals went in two by two: Take turns choosing the animals and make the animals walk up your child's back and down their arms. Big heavy elephant feet, little scuttling mice feet, scratchy polar bear claws, slow then speedy lion's paws – the possibilities are endless!

A made-up story about them: Take them on a journey where they are the main character. If you are super inventive, you can create your own story, but if, like me, you find that challenging, no plot is necessary – just travel through a variety of terrains, each of which has different moves to do. For example: John went on a journey, he went first through the swishy grass, then across the flowing river on the stepping stones. He jumped from stone to stone, oops he fell into the water – splash – and waded through the mud to the shore... If your memory (with their help) is up to it, once you reach the end, travel backwards through the journey.

All about me: Spell their name out on their back, or hand. Get them to do it for you too. You can also do their age, birth date, birth month or use details for other family members, including pets!

My pets: Do the actions that your pets do but use your hands to simulate them on your child's body. When our kids were little, we had a dog, cats, a hamster, and some fish. We did swish tails and a licky tongue for the dogs, leaps and pounces for the cats, scampery feet and chubby cheeks for the hamster, and splashy water and swooping dives for the fish. You do not have to have any pets for this – make them up, be as creative as you like. Who says you cannot have a Gruffalo, a dinosaur or a unicorn for a pet!

Fun massage games – for any age
What we did today (or will do tomorrow): Go through the actions of the activities for a day – walking, running, writing, eating with a knife and fork, driving the car round the bends. Use whatever you did or are going to do, using motion and touch as well as words.

Pizza toppings: Create a pizza from scratch on their body. Knead the dough using fingers squeezing together over their skin. Spread on the tomato sauce with flat hands making wide circles. Sprinkle on the cheese with tapping fingers. Then add lots of toppings – work together to choose the toppings. Things like pepperoni (big flat hands), scatters of red pepper or sweetcorn, lumps of chicken. Then the pizza goes into the oven and all the cheese melts with flat hands making wide circles again. Once it is cooked, you can slice it up with the pizza cutter!

What will the weather be? Make the motions of different weather on their body: light rain, heavy rain, warm sun, hailstones, thunder and lightning. Blow a breeze on their neck. Make a tornado, twisting across them, or a tidal wave over their shoulders.

Planting a garden: Make the flowers grow up their back and up over their head. Make some creatures visit, such as buzzing bees, fluttering butterflies, wiggly worms or even spiders. You can water the garden and blow a wind on the flowers too.

Gentle touching releases the body's feel-good chemicals and will reduce our children's stress levels. The physical connection reinforces the mental connection and strengthens the bond between us. It relaxes us too, so everyone wins!

— Chapter 3 —

STRENGTHENING COMMUNICATION

Good communication is the foundation of all healthy relationships and is essential for learning and play. Communication is often seen to be about making a point clearly, about conveying a message, but this is only half the story. Communication is a two-way process involving listening as well as talking.

When we have good communication with our child, it helps them develop skills for communicating not just with us, but with others too. It builds the relationship and sends the message that we value their thoughts and feelings. Working on communication skills can be hard at first, especially if some of the ways of talking and listening are different from how you were parented. Like all skills, practising helps. When you slip up, repair it with your child and start fresh. It's fine, no one always gets it right, and making changes takes time and effort. Try doing things a little at a time and before you know it, it will be second nature.

Non-verbal communication

Much communication happens without speech. Our gestures, facial expressions and posture communicate feelings without using any words. Long before they can talk, babies are communicating. They cry when they are hungry or sleepy or wet. They point to objects that they want and hold things out for us to take. We engage with them in a back-and-forth interaction which will develop over time into verbal conversation.

Where a caregiver is attuned to a baby, when the baby holds something out or points, the carer interacts; they may say thank you, they may name and describe the object. They are modelling turn-taking and joint attention. Babies have a natural desire to communicate, and when we use body language and gestures along with our words it helps them to understand what we are saying. When we smile, clap and show pleasure, it makes them feel good and encourages them to learn more. For children who have not had a positive start in life, whose caregivers may have been inconsistent in their responses, frequently ignoring or not noticing their cues, these rich development opportunities may have been missed and they may also have learned alternative strategies to gain attention. They may not realize that communication comes from more than words.

Our children may not have had enough of these early interactions, but we can fill in the gaps. By showing our children positive non-verbal communication, we strengthen the relationship and show our children that they are loved. Modelling positive, non-verbal behaviour helps our children to relate to others, understand social cues and build good relationships throughout their lives. By using warm and caring body language towards our children, we help them learn how to express love, and every time we stop and listen when our child wants to talk, we show them how to give other people attention. Here are a few practical things you can do one to one with your child, or as a family, to build on their non-verbal communication:

Send a positive message: Get down to their level and turn to face them as you talk to them or play with them. This helps them to feel secure and shows them that they have your undivided attention. Perhaps touch their arm or ruffle their hair if that is something they are comfortable with. Mirror their feelings and actions. For example, if they smile at you, then smile back. If they are a bit slumped and sad, sit like that too. Tone of voice is an important part of non-verbal communication too. Use a calm and friendly tone of voice allied with a relaxed posture and expression when you talk with them. This sends a positive message and shows them that you are there for them.

Match your actions to your words: Make sure that your body language matches what you are saying. For example, smiling and turning towards your child when you say 'Good morning' sends a clear message that you are happy to see them. But if your non-verbal communication does not match your words, it sends a mixed message. For example, if you ask your child a question and then turn away, your child will think you are not really interested in their answer. When your child says or does something funny that you do not want them to keep doing, it can be hard to match your non-verbal communication to your words. For example, calling their brother a poo-poo-head, or running into the room shrieking and naked when you have guests. It is tempting to laugh, but that sends them a mixed message. If you can, keep a straight face and say something like, 'In this family we speak politely to each other' or, 'It's after your bedtime, can I get you a drink and come and tuck you in?'

React to their cues: Children send us non-verbal cues all the time too. A toddler might hide behind you or cover their ears at a party to show that they are overwhelmed; an older child might touch their neck when they are nervous. Notice their non-verbal cues and respond to them. When you respond to your child's cues, you build a strong and supportive relationship where they feel loved and understood. For example, 'You're very quiet this afternoon. Did something happen at school?' or, 'Your voice is quite loud, and you are talking fast. I wonder if you are feeling a bit overwhelmed? Shall we go on the trampoline and bounce all the stress out?'

Point out examples: Use things that happen around you to highlight how what we see tells us how others are feeling. For example, 'That little girl looks a bit sad. Her shoulders are down, and she is looking at the ground' or, 'John looked a bit scared when you ran towards him. Did you see how his eyes went big and he stepped back?' or, 'I could see how happy you were as soon as you came through the door; you were smiling and skipping towards me'. Drawing their attention to non-verbal signals and deciphering helps them to notice and respond appropriately to the cues of others. Explain to your child that body movements and gestures alone don't always convey the whole picture. Your child needs to factor in tone of voice and words to get the full meaning of what someone is saying. Teachers might cross their arms because they are fed up, but it might just be because they are cold. A classmate could turn away because they aren't interested, or they might have heard a noise and are looking to see what it is. Help them to see the whole picture.

When talking isn't an option: Non-verbal communication can be helpful when you are somewhere noisy or are too far away to talk. At a soft play area, you might give your child a smile and a 'thumbs up' to check in with them, or high hand clapping, or blow a kiss when they do well in the school play. If they are doing something that looks as if it is not going well, you could shake your head or hold a hand up to signal that they should stop.

Have fun acting it out: Choose a feeling and act it out while commentating on the unspoken messages behind what you are doing. Don't do lots at once as this can be a bit overwhelming; just do one at a time. Choose a moment where that emotion comes up, perhaps make it a joke. For example, if your child is taking a while to get ready to go out you could act out being impatient. 'Look how impatient I am! My fingers are tapping, my hands are on my hips.' Make it light and fun as an easy way to get the information across. Fitting things into everyday events is a great way to build on your child's learning without it seeming as if you are instructing them.

Learning from TV: When you watch TV together, look for the body language that is conveying the emotion. Help your child spot cues that indicate how each person is feeling. Pause and rewind if you can and watch it again. Say out loud what you are seeing and your interpretation of this. For example, 'The man was looking away when she was talking. I don't think he was listening' or, 'Her face looked a bit red, and her fists were clenched. I think she was cross with him.' Talk together about the cues you are seeing that are helping you to work it out. You can even watch TV with the sound off and see if you can guess what is happening and what the people are feeling.

Body language charades: Pick a simple sentence such as, 'I would like more potatoes' or, 'What time is it?' and act it out in different ways to convey an emotion. Try being sad or grumpy or excited. The body language and tone of voice changes but the words stay the same. The other person (or people) can guess how the person speaking is feeling.

Working with our child to notice and understand the unspoken communication around them improves their communication with us and the wider world and it strengthens our connection to them.

Learning to listen, listening to learn

All too often in our interaction with our children we are not listening to what they say. We make assumptions based on what we ourselves think, or what we believe that our children think. We may think that because they are experiencing something that we have already experienced, they feel exactly how we did. Or we may assume that because they behaved in a certain way last year, that is still how they will feel and react today.

How we see the world and react to it is based on our life experiences and the pathways that these experiences have built up in our brains. No two people will react in the same way to the same experience. Children who have experienced early life trauma might respond quite differently from how we might react, or how we might expect them to react.

Our children will not think as we do, they will not experience something in the same way that we did, but will think and experience things in their own way. The only way to understand how our children are feeling and why they are behaving as they do, is to listen to them. We must stop mind reading and really try to understand what they are feeling and why, rather than second-guessing.

Sometimes our children can react and behave in ways that seem illogical to us, but they are following patterns that are logical for them. When we take the time to understand where they are coming from, it makes sense. For example:

- The three-year-old who consistently wet herself at nursery at lunchtime when she was successfully dry the rest of the time. To an adult brain this seems illogical, but in her mind, she was too scared to go to the toilet because she knew that Mummy would come soon. She was worried that if she was not in the room when Mummy came, she would leave without her.
- The nine-year-old who kept bothering the dog despite being told to leave her in peace as she had just had a stroke. To an adult mind this could seem like disobedient behaviour; however, in the child's mind, he had heard the vet say it was like the dog was 'dizzy' and to him this meant it was just like when you spin round in the garden and you feel dizzy for a bit, then it is all okay. Although he had previously seen that the dog was very unwell, once he heard that she was 'dizzy' he thought it was nothing to worry about. By understanding the child's thought process, the

adults were able to help him to realize what the reality was, and his behaviour towards the dog immediately changed.

- The ten-year-old who could not wait to share the 'good news' that her Aunt and Uncle had split up – because now there was a spare ticket for her to go to see the X Factor live. To the adult mind this may seem heartless and incredibly narcissistic of the child. However, for her, the ramifications for her family were not apparent, and her attention was firmly focused on the excitement of getting to go to the X Factor. All that she could see was the windfall for her.

We can all be guilty of stepping in and prompting our children, telling them what they are feeling. We need to give them the time and space to respond. It is good to sit quietly and patiently and wait. It can seem like a long time but resist the temptation to fill the space with chatter. Children can require twice as much, or more, time to process information as adults, so remember to give them space to think and time to answer. Tune in to your child's conversational style. Are they a lively, energetic talker or are they slower and more reflective? Are they chattier in the morning, or the afternoon? Respect their natural style and rhythms and connect with them in their way at their pace.

To communicate with our children, we need to take the time to really listen to what they are saying so that we can understand things from their point of view. It is the linguistic equivalent of getting to their eye level when they are small. Once you start listening and asking your child about how they see the world, it is amazing what fantastic conversations you can have. The reality our children inhabit inside their heads is a magical, many layered place, and as adults we have a lot to learn from understanding their take on things.

When we truly listen to our children, we can understand their viewpoint and their motives. With understanding comes acceptance. The more we accept our children, the more accepted they feel and the more confident they feel about themselves and their opinions. Delving into their perspective on the world not only opens up your child's viewpoint to you, but also provides incredible opportunities to bond and creates shared memories which bolster feelings of belonging and self-worth in your child. When we respect how they see the world, we respect, understand and accept them for the special and unique people that they are.

Active listening

Active listening is key to effective communication and shows your child that you care and are interested in them, which deepens and strengthens the relationship. It can also help you learn about your child's perspective and understand more about what is going on in their life.

Show that you are listening by how your body reacts. Turn towards them or lean in to them, face them and, if they are comfortable with it, make eye contact. Make encouraging noises and use words like 'Really...' 'Go on...' to show that you want them to continue. Build on what they are telling you and show your interest by saying things like, 'Tell me more about...' Repeat or rephrase their words every so often. This reinforces that you are listening and helps you check that you have understood. Try not to jump in or finish their sentences, give them time to process what they want to say. Let them finish talking before you respond, and when you do talk, use language and ideas that they will understand.

As they talk, watch their facial expressions and body language for clues on how they are feeling. Listening is not just about hearing words, but also about trying to understand what is going on behind those words. When they are describing something that has emotional content, prompt them to think about how they are feeling by describing what you think they may be feeling. For example, 'It sounds like you felt left out in the park when the other kids went off to play on the climbing frame'. It is fine to get it wrong; in fact, that gives your child the opportunity to reflect and decide for themselves what they were feeling. Your child might just want you to listen, so do not rush to resolve their problems; give them space to reflect for themselves and to feel that their feelings and point of view matter.

When you listen to your child you show them that you care and model good listening, which develops their listening skills too. When you talk respectfully with your child and others, this reinforces positive communication.

How it feels to be heard

When you have empathy with someone, you tune into what they are feeling and are sensitive to their point of view. You do not have to agree with what they are saying, but you do have to accept that it is how they feel. It is essential for our children's sense of self-worth that they feel heard and understood; that they feel we accept their position and empathize with their feelings. When a child feels heard it diffuses the emotion, removes the confrontation and therefore a more rational conversation can be held. When they do not feel heard, it will descend very quickly into argument and entrenched positions.

For example, imagine that your child comes home from school and says, 'I had a horrid day at school. My teacher held me back to tell me off and then I missed most of break.'

How would they feel if you said, 'What did you do to get told off? I am sure if the teacher was annoyed with you, you deserved it. Why can't you behave properly in class?' How might they react?

Or, how would they feel if you said, 'You seem really upset. It sounds like today was a tough day for you. How disappointing to miss break. Do you want to talk about it?' How might they react?

Which response would you prefer if you were the child?

Can you think of any times when you felt that your feelings were not respected? How did you feel about the other person? How did you react?

Learning to empathize with our children is essential; it gives them a feeling of being heard, which in turn builds self-worth. It also helps them to grow into adults who respect, understand and empathize with others.

Mind your language

If we want our children to respect us and understand us, we need to communicate clearly. We do our best to achieve this, but even with the greatest intentions, we get tired, stressed and cross and don't always get our message across in the way that we intended. There are a few simple things that we can do to make ourselves better understood and to help our children to frame their language in a more positive way too.

Use 'I' messages

It is all too easy when we do not like what our children are doing to use statements where we are blaming them for what we feel:

- You are making too much noise, you are giving me a headache.
- You are making me angry!
- You have made me sad.
- You are so messy.
- You are not making any sense.

We can all remember times when someone has blamed us for something. It feels unpleasant, and it puts us on the defensive so that we either come out fighting or retreat into ourselves. No one reacts well to being blamed.

When we change from using 'you' to using 'I', we defuse the language. When we use an 'I' statement we are taking responsibility for our own feelings and taking the pressure off our children.

So instead of blaming them, own it yourself:

- When it is so noisy it gives me a headache and I feel a bit cross.
- I feel disappointed when you break things that belong to me.
- I feel sad when you two argue with each other.
- I do not understand; can you explain that again?

Some tips for effective 'I' messages:

- Keep your words, voice and expression consistent with the intensity of your feelings.
- Be clear and specific. Talk about what is happening now, not in the past.
- Do not use all-encompassing words like 'always' and 'never'.
- If the feeling that you want to express is anger, keep in mind that anger is a secondary emotion; it can be more effective to use words that describe the feelings underlying the anger such as frustration or disappointment. Anger often breeds more anger and defensiveness.

Use more 'dos' than 'don'ts'

Clear your mind. Think of anything you want to, anything except a large pink elephant raising its trunk. Is your mind clear? Or are you picturing a large pink elephant?

The reason we find this so hard is because of how our brains work. To understand not doing something, our brain first creates a picture of what it is that we are not meant to do. This picture can then influence us to do it. Salespeople use these embedded commands to plant suggestions in the minds of their customers.

Have you ever had an experience where you ask your child to do something, and they do the opposite? It happens all the time. If we focus on what we have asked, we might find the reason.

For example:

- Do not touch that.
- Stop running.
- Do not fall off.
- Do not be so rough with that.
- Stop shouting.
- You will break it.
- Do not play with the light switch.
- Do not sit on the stairs.
- Do not leave your shoes lying about.
- You should not talk with your mouth full.

We use embedded commands all the time without realizing it. Children hear a lot of 'don'ts.' As parents we often focus on what we do not want to happen, and, like the pink elephant, this can reinforce the behaviour that we do not want to see. To get a positive outcome, we need to avoid using instructions which are stating what we do not want, and instead focus on the desired outcome – the one we want.

For example:

- This is hot, stay over there while I put it back in the oven.
- Come down carefully and watch where you place your feet.
- Be gentle with that.
- That is fragile, put it down gently.
- Put the light on so we can see to read the story.
- Come into the sitting room where there is more room to play.
- Put your shoes on the shoe rack.
- Finish eating before you talk, so I can understand what you are saying.

Next time you catch yourself thinking or saying 'Don't...' 'Stop...', 'You cannot...', 'You shouldn't...' think of what you can usefully and safely encourage your child to do instead. If you *do* say 'Don't...', then it is okay to immediately follow it up with what it is you do want them to do.

Avoid limiting language

Is the language you and your children use working for you, or sabotaging you and setting you up for failure? When we look in detail at our words, it is easy to see how quickly we can undermine ourselves.

How often do you hear your child (or yourself) say statements such as:

- I can't cycle for more than 20 minutes.
- I'm no good at ball sports.
- If I tried that, I'd get it wrong and make a fool of myself.
- I will never be able to do that.

So how about reframing the statement so it is not limiting our behaviour? Making a small change to the language we use makes a big difference to the effect we have:

- I can cycle for up to 20 minutes.
- I have had some challenges with ball sports.
- I have never tried it before but I'm willing to give it a go.
- Until now I haven't been able to achieve this.

Listen closely to the words your children use, and to your own thoughts and words to see how often you use limiting language to restrict what you can and cannot do. When you recognize limiting language, help them (or yourself) to say it another way. By changing the language that we use, we can change a flat-out dismissal into a possibility, something we could have a go at. It opens doors to all sorts of new options and new experiences.

Assume success

How can we (or our children) have the courage to take on new things if we keep telling ourselves we might not succeed? When we ask our children to try to do something, we are opening the door to the idea that they might not be able to. We say things like try to remember your homework diary, try to write neatly, try to do your piano practice before bed. When we do this, our intentions are good. We often use 'try', thinking that it is softening the statement and reducing the pressure on our children. If you really want something, then go for it. Do not 'try' to achieve it.

Instead of asking your children to try, ask them to succeed. When we ask our children to try to do something, we imply that they might not manage, we assume that they will not succeed. We sow the seeds in their mind that they probably won't manage to do it.

For example:

- Remember your homework diary.
- Write on the lines, it helps to make it neater.
- Make sure that you have time to do your piano practice before bed.
- I know you will do your best.

It is important to stress that you are not putting pressure on them by doing this, it is just a much clearer way of saying what you want, and it reinforces your child's belief that they can do it. The point is not to banish the word 'try' from your vocabulary, just to notice and stop using it in places where it limits your child.

THINK before you speak

The following technique (or variations of it) is used in many schools as a way of helping children to think of the language that they are using and the effect it has on others.

Focus on your own words and encourage your children to **THINK** before they speak – to ask themselves is it True, Helpful, Inspiring, Necessary or Kind?

This also gives you a way to point out when they do not interact in a positive way by asking, 'Was that true, helpful, inspiring, necessary or kind? What could you have done instead?'

In our house, we use an abbreviated version much of the time, asking if it was 'kind, helpful or necessary'. This was what was used at our children's school so it was consistent with what they heard there and was less for the adults to remember in the heat of the moment.

Use kind words

In the hubbub of family life, it can be easy to get caught up in patterns where the way we speak to each other is not positive or supportive. We can slip into communication that ridicules or shames. Statements like 'You're acting like a toddler', 'Stop embarrassing me' or 'Don't be stupid' leave a child feeling put down and rejected. Respect for themselves and others starts with the way we speak to each other within the family.

There are lots of moments to say kind things throughout the day. Seek out opportunities to let your child know that you love them, and they are deserving of that love.

For example:

- That shirt really suits you. It makes your eyes look even more blue than usual.
- You were concentrating so hard on your picture. Well done.
- It was lovely to see how nicely you played with your friends.
- Great sharing.
- You are so kind.
- Thank you for helping with the dishes.
- These cakes are delicious. You could go on *Bake Off* when you grow up.

Inside and outside thoughts

It can be challenging for children to understand what it is okay to say and what it is not. And when impulse control is difficult, it can be easy for children to blurt things out that cause upset and get in the way of making friends.

A helpful way to approach this is to use the concept of inside and outside thoughts, to get children thinking how we all have all sorts of thoughts in our heads and that even if the thoughts are mean, they are only thoughts. We all have mean thoughts sometimes, it's what we do with those thoughts that counts. Talking about all the different thoughts we have in our heads helps us to explore with our children when they can verbalize their thoughts and when they can't; to think before they speak about whether their words will make someone else feel sad, angry or upset, or whether they might get someone else in trouble or make the person not want to be their friend. They need to reflect on whether the thought should stay inside their head or is okay to say out loud for others to hear.

For example, in a school setting some inside thoughts might be: *I do not like her; his drawing is rubbish; I don't want to work with a girl; he is not doing what the teacher told him; he was talking when the teacher was out of class.* Some outside thoughts might be: *I need help; I am worried about something; I like your pencil case.*

Talking through a particular issue or situation can help a child to understand and learn how to make different choices in the future.

Be curious and encourage curiosity

Conversations can be planned and deliberate, but many of the best chats happen in the moments in between: walking or driving to school, bath time, bedtime. The common denominator in many of these moments is that you are alongside your child. There is something freeing about not looking at each other. Being parallel to each other opens channels for conversation and in these moments you are both present for each other for the time that the journey, bath or bedtime lasts.

Take these opportunities to talk about everyday things as you go through your day. Involve your child in adult conversations, ask their opinion. If you and your child are used to communicating a lot, it can make it easier to talk when big or tricky issues come up. Be willing to stop what you are doing and listen to your child. Often you cannot predict when your child will start talking about something important to them.

Ask open questions

Closed questions are questions that have a yes or no response, whereas open questions encourage a fuller answer. Both are useful, however, when we want to encourage communication with our children. Open questions encourage them to think more deeply and allow them to add more information to their answer and to understand better. They also provide our children with the opportunity to explain or describe something, which develops their language skills, expands their vocabulary and exercises their memory.

Ask questions such as:

- What did you do today at school?
- How did you make these cakes? What ingredients did you use?
- What can you tell me about your favourite TV programme?
- What would happen if...
- What do you think about...
- In what way...
- Tell me about...
- What happened next?

- How can we...
- What would you do...
- How did you...
- What caused that to happen do you think?

Start open questions with how, what, when, who or where. Avoid using 'why' when asking personal questions as it can sound critical or judgemental. So instead of saying, 'Why did you do that?' ask, 'What happened?'

Show your interest

These statements encourage your child to say more because they show that you are interested. They communicate that you think their feelings, thoughts and ideas are important.

- Wow.
- I see.
- Oh.
- How about that!
- Really?
- Tell me more.
- That's interesting.
- Amazing.

When you use these statements along with giving your full attention and looking at them, your child will know that you are listening. Children are more likely to share when they sense that you are engaged with what they're saying.

Ask clean questions

Clean questions are used by counsellors when working with clients to ask questions about their world without prompting or putting their own perspective on it. They can be helpful for parents too, as they help us to ask questions without adding our own interpretation and meaning to what our children are trying to say. They are clean of emotion or judgement and help our children to express themselves, and us to understand their point of view.

Here are some examples of clean questions:

- What's important to you about that?
- What will it be like when you have it? What will be different?
- What does that mean to you?
- Is there anything else about it?

Reflect their words back to them in the questions by replacing 'that' and 'it' with their own words.

Use yourself as a conversation starter

If we want our children to open up and talk about their day, then it's helpful if we do the same. It takes the pressure off them. It can also help them to remember things that happened and share them. For example, 'Joan at work was really cross today, she was very snappy in our meeting' might prompt your child to remember something similar in their day. It's also an opportunity to model positive reactions to things that happen. For example, an anecdote such as, 'I used the self-service checkout in the supermarket today and it kept beeping and saying I needed the assistant. I felt a bit embarrassed and flustered, so I did some counting and breathing to calm down' helps our children to see that things go wrong, and we all get flustered, but when we do, there are things we can do to help ourselves regulate.

Asking big questions

The more we talk to our kids, the better they are at understanding the world and problem-solving. Asking fun questions can be a great way to start conversations.

Here are a few examples to try out:

- What do you think you are going to dream about tonight?
- If your teddy could talk, what would he say?
- What's the difference between grown-ups and children? Which would you rather be?
- Did you get a chance to help anyone today? And did anyone help you today?
- If you could give everyone in the family new names, what would they be and why?
- What is your superhero name and what are your powers?

- If you could ask an animal a question, what animal would you ask and what question?
- Why do you think it's important that friends, family and neighbours help each other?
- Have you ever had to be brave?
- Can you think of a helpful thing you wish you had done today?
- Today I heard this on the news. I wonder how it felt to be there? I wonder how we can help?
- What is one thing you are grateful for today?
- Can you think of one act of kindness you would like to do tomorrow?
- Did anything confuse you today? Maybe I can help you to make sense of it.
- What are you proud of today?
- If you won the lottery, how would you spend the money?
- If you won the lottery and couldn't spend the money on yourself or our family, how would you spend it?
- If you could only keep one toy, what would it be? And who would you give the rest to?
- If you could change one thing in the world, what would you change?

Do not expect too much though. More often than not you will get little or no response, but every so often you will spark something which will bring out the creativity and big heart inside your child and it will all be worthwhile.

Creating time for curiosity

Children are endlessly curious about the world and often they ask big questions when we are right in the middle of something else. Even though we may not have the time at the point when they are asking, we do not want to discourage this wonderful curiosity. How about creating a curiosity jar to put the questions into? Then when you have more time, you can dip in and investigate together.

Encouraging yes rather than no

Every day there are multiple times when we need to ask or tell our children to do something. At the same time, our children have their own wants and needs which are sometimes in direct conflict with what we want them to do. Our children may feel a need to control to feel safe and may struggle with transitions. No matter how skilfully we ask, as parents we will hear the word 'no' a lot. This can feel frustrating when we are rushed, stressed or tired and we just want to get things done. It is all too easy to respond by forcing the issue, making it more of a struggle. This can lead to a joint escalation, where you each keep reacting more strongly and it can quickly turn into a confrontation. Or the opposite can happen where we give in, which escalates things in a different way.

When we are in confrontation with our children, neither of us gets what we want, and the relationship can be damaged. When we find a way to work together, we both get what we want and in the shared experience we build connection and help our children to feel safe and loved.

How do we increase cooperation and keep the connection strong, while still achieving what we need?

Connect, then get their attention: If your child is focused on something else, it can be difficult to shift their attention on to you. If you can, wait until another time, or if it must be now, connect with them first. Ask about what they are doing, focus on it for a moment to get their attention on to you. Start by moving in close and going down to their level, using their name or a greeting to get their attention. Use a calm, clear voice and when you do ask them to do something, ask them to repeat back what you asked them to do.

Ask where possible, keeping telling to a minimum: When we do need to get them to do a particular thing, we can either ask them or tell them to do it. When you make a request, you are asking, and your child can choose to say yes or no. When you tell your child to do something, you instruct them what to do and when. There is no choice, they do not have the option to say no. Instructions and requests are both important; however, use more requests as these give your child choices and a sense of control, which might make them more likely to cooperate. Use instructions when it is important that your child does as you say, for example, 'Hold my hand while we cross the road.' Keep them to a minimum though, as children can feel overwhelmed or that they have no control if there are too many instructions.

Make it clear and give a reason: Whether you are asking or telling, make the language as clear and age appropriate as possible to ensure that they understand what you are saying. Children often need reminders, so be prepared to repeat yourself. Make it clear and give a reason for asking. For example, 'Do you want to wear your hat? It is cold outside' or, 'Can you pick up your cars from the table because I need to set it for tea.'

Use when...then statements: Ally your request with another activity that your child wants to do: 'When you have put all your Lego away, then we can go to Mary's house.'

Say what you want: Say what you want rather than what you do not want. For example, say, 'Please keep all four legs of the chair on the ground' rather than, 'Don't rock the chair.' Try adding an incentive that will encourage them to do what you are asking them to do. For example, 'If you can put your shoes on quickly, we'll have more time at the park' or, 'If you tidy up your toys quickly, we will have time to make the cakes.'

Ask in a creative way: Use a question rather than an instruction; for example, rather than, 'Hang your coat up' ask, 'Where does your coat go?' Or describe what you see rather than using an instruction; for example, instead of, 'Put your socks in the laundry basket' say, 'I see socks on the floor.' Doing things in a different way gets their attention and lessens the demand.

Give notice: Where a transition is going to happen, for example leaving for school, give notice ahead of time so your child knows what is happening. Using a timer can help as it takes the pressure off you to remember and gives your children a visual reminder.

Give a closed choice: Instead of asking them to do something, give them a choice of what to do while they do it. For example, instead of saying, 'Please can you come for your bath' say, 'It's bath time, do you want bubbles? Or no bubbles?' Or instead of asking them to get dressed, say, 'It's time to get dressed, do you want the blue t-shirt or the red one?' This increases the chances of your child doing what you ask, because it gives them some choice, but the choice contains within it the implication that they will do the thing you are asking.

Keep demands to a minimum: Think about how many demands are being put on your child. Traditional parenting has a core belief that children should do as they are told, and the consequences of noncompliance are blame or punishment. All the power is with the adult and none with the child. This removes any right of choice from the child and if they do not comply, their choice is between submission and rebellion. It can be easy to slip into this familiar way of parenting, to repeat patterns of how we were parented and put lots of demands on our children believing that it is our job to tell our children what to do. However, no one responds well to demands and they reduce connection. Sometimes demands will be necessary, to keep our child safe, for example, but try to keep them to a minimum and instead bring your child onside in a way that encourages them to feel that they have choices.

Build in success: A helpful strategy is to set things up for your child to succeed. If your child struggles with transitions, then lessen the feeling of change and give them some choices and control. For example, if you want to get your child to come out on a walk, although they enjoy this activity, they may have previously refused to put their boots on or taken ages or refused to get ready when you asked them directly. What if you tried a softer approach with smaller steps rather than one large transition? Perhaps start by getting them to pick a snack to take; then to put the snack in their jacket pocket as they put it on; then to decide where to walk. Hand over some control to them in the little steps. Then do the boots once they have already bought in to the idea of a walk. Smooth the transition to get a yes.

Use natural consequences: Think about whether you need to tell them to do something. Could you ask instead and if they do not do it, will there be a natural consequence that they could learn from for themselves? For example, if they do not put a coat on to go out in the garden, will they get cold and realize they need a coat? Or if you ask them to put a snack in their bag, and they do not, they will realize at break when they do not have one, which will help them to remember the next time. The more we let them learn for themselves, the more they will manage to do for themselves.

Blame a third party: Take the pressure off you by explaining that they need to do it because someone (or something) other than you says they should. For example, 'You have to wear a seatbelt, it's the law' or, 'The physiotherapist said you needed to do your exercises every day.' Timers can be helpful for this too, as it appears that the timer is saying it is time to stop rather than a parent.

Make it a game: Often we can achieve what we want by making it a game. For example, if you want your child to tidy up their toys, see how many they can pick up in five minutes. Or make it a competition between siblings. This lessens the feeling of demand on our children and helps us feel calmer too.

Use one-word reminders: If you do need to remind them, use a shortened version, such as 'Hands!' instead of 'Have you washed your hands?'

Model saying yes: Say yes whenever you can. For example, 'Can I have a biscuit?' 'Yes, after lunch' or, 'Can we play a game', 'Yes once I finish this email in ten minutes. You get the game set up and I will join you.'

Ask as a favour: 'Could you help and let the dogs out while I make the pizza?' or, 'Could you do me a favour and get your PE kit so I can wash it?' This encourages their sense of importance and responsibility.

Highlight their strengths: 'Could you help me look for the car keys? You are so good at spotting things' or, 'Can you help me hose down the garden chairs? You are so much better than me at spotting all the grubby bits.' This highlights their strengths and makes them feel good.

Ask questions to encourage self-discovery: Are you telling them when in fact you could use the opportunity to ask questions to encourage them to learn for themselves? Ask rather than tell. Ask questions that enable them to see for themselves why something happens, or what to do and when.

We had a notable example of this with our son learning to swim. His swimming teacher was working with him at his lesson, and I watched the teacher keep telling my son to hold the float in a particular way when they were practising leg kicks. Over and over my son got it wrong, or changed his grip, and over and over the teacher told him how to hold it. At the end of the lesson, the teacher was disappointed as he felt my son was not listening. My son felt bad about himself and was frustrated as he felt he was not doing what he should be doing and could not seem to do what the teacher wanted. Neither teacher nor pupil enjoyed the lesson, and his swimming did not improve. In fact, the reverse happened as he felt so demotivated.

My husband took our son swimming later in the week and I mentioned what had happened at the lesson. His dad chose to *ask* questions rather than *tell* him what to do. He got him to play about with the float, holding it in different ways and pushing it through the water. Each time he asked lots of questions: How does that feel? Is it hard to push or easy? Is it easy to hold onto like that or difficult? How does your body feel when you hold it that way? Through asking these questions, our son understood for himself what felt right and what felt wrong. He thought about it and worked out what the right way to hold the float was based on what he learned. After that, he understood and wanted to hold the float in the right way for it to be streamlined and aid his swimming practice. His dad empowered him to do it for himself and he came out of the pool feeling great about himself.

What are they saying yes to? It can be useful to think about what is going on for our child when we ask or tell them to do something; to think about what is behind their no. Is there perhaps something that they are saying yes to? For example, saying no to playing with a sibling might be saying yes to quiet time with a book. Or saying no to leaving the park means they are having fun with their friends. Validate their feelings: 'I can see you want to stay at the park and are disappointed, but remember, we will be back tomorrow, and we have to go now to get home in time for tea.' Having empathy with their reasons gives us insights which can frame our next move. Sometimes we might be okay with the no, other times we will not. Sometimes it will be possible for us to choose to change when we ask, and pick a time when they are more likely to agree. When we empathize with our children, we make a connection, they feel heard and understood, and they are more able to work out a solution that meets everyone's needs. 'No' can be an opportunity to learn about our child, to see other options and to build connections.

If your child is not cooperating, it might be because you are expecting more than they are able to do, or because they feel unwell, tired or anxious. They may go through phases where they just want to say no. Behaviours change as they develop and practise independence. This is normal. Try to be consistent, firm and loving and prioritize getting your child to cooperate on the important things, like safety.

Chapter 4

STRUCTURE AND ROUTINE

Consistency and structure are helpful for all children; however, they are especially important for children who have experienced inconsistent and chaotic care in their early lives. Creating clear structure and expectations for our children provides a framework within which they can feel safe – a framework where the world feels more predictable, where they are clear not only on what happens next, but how the adults will respond too.

When we are consistent, we follow through. We have clear boundaries which are not open to negotiation. This provides a sense of safety and security for our children. Being consistent is different from being strict; it is not about control, it is measured and predictable and is about connection and safety.

Even though we may seek to create structure and predictability in our children's lives, unexpected changes will happen. When this occurs, our children can become anxious and fear that their safety and security are under threat. Having routine and consistency as the backbone in their lives means that when things change, they will be more able to adapt.

Some of us love to have a daily routine, while others prefer spontaneity. In times of stress and change we may feel the need for structure in our lives more than at other times, as maintaining structure and routine can make us feel more organized and in control. Similarly, children whose early life experiences have been chaotic and unpredictable need an environment where things are consistent. They need homes where there is structure and routine to make the world seem a safer and more predictable place. Brains that developed without a sense of the world as a safe place can be fearful when things are new or when plans change. Sometimes the difference can seem tiny to us but may feel huge to our child.

Creating a framework

Having structure and routine in the day helps our child (and us) know who will be doing what, where it will be, with whom, when and for how long. It creates a framework of predictability and familiarity that supports children to feel safe. Routines make each day run a little more smoothly and can help us all through the challenging parts of our day.

Routines can be created for the things that happen every day, such as getting ready for school, mealtimes, or bedtime, but are also helpful for things that happen weekly, such as going to a swimming lesson, going to after-school club or going out for the day, or things that happen infrequently, like Christmas or going on holiday. Routines can be helpful for times when things regularly go awry; times like going to the supermarket, on a long drive, or visiting family or friends. Routines help our children to feel safe and secure and this puts them in a better place to learn and develop confidence.

Create a simple pictorial or textual representation of an activity, of a timeslot, of the day or of the week. Tailor the amount of text to your child – the younger the child, the more pictures. Help your child to see that there is order in the world. You do not need anything special to do this. There are a lot of images available online if you choose to build it on a computer, or in magazines if you wish to do it on paper. Doing it on a computer can be helpful as it allows you to make the images specific to them – their pyjamas, their socks or pictures of them doing some of the activities. Make it as personal as you can and involve your child in the creation. Make them part of the process and get their understanding and buy-in as you do. Creating this structure and predictability means your child knows what to expect and this frees them from worrying about what might happen.

Once you have a completed routine, put it up somewhere that it is easy to see and on hand when your child needs to see it. For example, the getting ready for school one could be in the kitchen or hall and the getting ready for bed one in their bedroom. When it is time for one of the routines, give them a prompt, for example, 'Time for your bedtime routine'. Initially you may need to take them through it and it will take time and support for a child to get used to a new routine. Sometimes it will only take days, but it can take a few weeks.

Bringing structure to the week

As adults, we will have calendars on our phones, on the wall, or in our pockets or bags – multiple ways that we order and plan our weeks. Our children do not have all of this at their disposal and do not require this level of complexity either. There are lots of ways to create a weekly schedule that is accessible to your child. You can do it on paper either by hand or digitally then print it off, or you can use a whiteboard. A whiteboard is a cheap, simple and flexible option as you can keep the recurring events on week after week and add/rub off any that are specific to that week. Having a central location at home where you and your child can see what is going on this week sparks conversation about what is happening and encourages your child to check for themselves too.

Daily routines

Children thrive when they know what to expect – even if they may not always like it. The mainstay of creating structure is a regular routine where the time we get up, eat meals and snacks, and go to bed is constant. In this predictability and sameness, our child can feel safer and more secure.

Creating this structure can feel strict and restrictive for us; however, this scaffold around them helps them to understand limits and boundaries and is what they need to enable them to flourish. Having routines also fosters independence and reduces conflict. When a child is used to their morning routine always involving breakfast, teeth-brushing, getting dressed, packing a bag and leaving for school, this becomes a given and the need for nagging and reminders is reduced. This sense of independence can in turn create self-confidence as your child becomes more able to take care of themselves.

You will know best how the day works for your family, and of course weekends will be different from school days. If your days currently have little defined structure, introduce it gradually in one part of the day at a time so as not to create an overwhelming level of change. Prioritize the demanding times in the day. Before school and bedtime are often stressful so can be a good place to start.

CREATING A MORNING ROUTINE

Think about all the things that your children do before school and the optimum order to do them in. Some of the activities like brushing teeth, washing hands and face and brushing hair are similar and linking these together can help your child remember them as they become associated in their minds. Make the complexity and level of text age appropriate. For example, single words rather than sentences may be better if your child finds reading challenging. Add pictures and make them personal to them if you can. On ours, we had pictures of them in their school uniform, of their bags with what would be packed inside them, of their favourite breakfast and of our car, to make the routine come to life and enable our children to see it as theirs.

CREATING STRUCTURE AT BEDTIME

A bedtime routine is a lovely way to end the day and help your child to regulate and prepare for sleep. Ensure that their bedroom is a safe, relaxing space. Think about all their senses while they sleep. How light is it? Does the room need a blackout blind? Would a night light help? What about adding a scent like lavender to their pillow? What about relaxing music playing? Or a recording of a story? There are lots of options available and you can even record yourself reading to make it personal. If your child likes pressure, would a weighted blanket help? Or tightly tucked sheets? Or a double duvet cover on a single bed tucked in to make a snug envelope? Or what about texture? Would they get comfort from something soft and fluffy? Or cool and cotton? Would they like a hot water bottle? Or a favourite toy or two? Tailor things to them, see it from their point of view and set things up to encourage them to succeed in sleeping well and independently.

In the hour before bed, set the scene for bed and move towards bed-time in a predictable way. Do things in the same order each night so your child knows what is coming next and can feel safe and secure. Include things like a snack or a drink, having a bath, teeth-brushing and going to the toilet. Take time to chat about the day and talk through things that happened, read a favourite story, look at pictures, sing a song or give them a massage. Play calm games like checking body parts, such as nose, chin, ears, cheeks, fingers, toes and knees, to see if they are warm/cold, hard/soft, wiggly/quiet, and so on. Count freckles, toes, fingers and knuckles.

Do things that are calm and that build the connection and bring comfort to your child and help them settle to sleep. Let your child know what is next in the routine, so they know what you expect them to do. For instance, 'After your bath, we'll get you dressed for bed.' This helps your child feel safe and secure and lets them know it is time to sleep. Once you have found a routine that suits you and your child, you can create a pictorial version of it that you can follow together. Having a physical representation cements the routine for your child and over time will foster independence.

The predictability of a bedtime routine will help create feelings of relaxation and comfort, tell their body it is time to sleep and help your child separate from you after a long day together. Finish with a goodnight kiss and say goodnight. If they do not want you to go, say you will be back to check on them in five minutes – and keep to your word. You can keep repeating this if they are still awake.

Building in predictability

When an adult creates organization and predictability by maintaining a regular time for meals and activities it gives children a feeling of safety and stability. Have some things that happen in the same way each day, such as a bedtime routine. Have a regular family movie night; build in structure to the week. Talk through the next day or what is going to happen next. Remember that food is nurture and helps to build attachment, so make time to have snacks together or try and bake something which you can all enjoy at snack time. When a child knows what to expect, the day will feel less stressful.

Plan ahead: When you are going somewhere new or going on holiday, help your child to familiarize with the place before you go. Look at pictures and videos online. If there is a journey, or several parts to the outing, then talk them through all the steps so that they know what is coming next.

Countdown to big events: Count down the sleeps to a big event to help your child know what is coming and get a sense of time passing. You can do this on a calendar, with a block counter or by printing off numbers to strike off each day.

Speak of the future and make plans: Often, children who have experienced trauma can see the future as scary, bleak and unpredictable. Talk about things you will do in the future, next month, next year, when they are older. Establish a sense of permanency and belonging in your words.

Keep your promises: You can build your child's ability to trust by showing them that you are trustworthy. Be consistent and follow through on what you say you are going to do. If you make promises, you need to keep them. However, if you say something in the heat of the moment that you know you will not follow through with, such as, 'No TV for the rest of the month', then own up to this and acknowledge it with your child. This shows that you are seeking to be consistent and models positive behaviour when a mistake is made.

Be flexible sometimes: Having structure does not mean that you cannot decide to throw the routine out of the window sometimes. Some of the best fun we have had as a family has been on nights where the children have stayed up late because we had visitors or were at friends' houses. One particularly late night a badger ran across the road in front of us on the walk home and the children were entranced. If you are going to deviate from the routine, do it in a planned way, make sure your child will cope with it, and explain why you are doing it and that it is a special day and that is why it is different.

Keep things age appropriate: Revisit how you do things periodically to make sure that they are still age appropriate for your child and that they are still serving you as a family.

Creating structure and predictability in our child's days will reduce the power struggles and help them to feel safer and more able to be independent.

Transitions

Change happens all the time, but this does not make it any easier for us or our children to manage. Structure and stability feel safe for children and changes at home, at school, in friendships and in the world around them can make life feel uncertain and that is an uncomfortable and often scary feeling. As our children navigate these changes, when we support them with their big feelings, we can enable them to learn coping strategies and develop resilience. When change is happening for our children, we too can feel uncertain, and this can feed into our children's fears, so the starting point to enable our children to regulate themselves is to regulate ourselves.

Children who have experienced trauma can be more sensitive to change. Their needs may have not been met in a consistent way and they may have had multiple major changes, separations and losses to deal with already in their lives. Experiencing this creates a brain focused on fear and uncertainty, which will find transitions more challenging.

We often see transition as only being about the big things in our children's lives. Changing teacher, changing school or moving house. These transitions have major impacts but there are also lots of tiny transitions every day that our children do that we may not recognize as being transitions.

A transition is defined as a move from one place, state or experience to another. When we think of it in that way, a transition can be something as small as moving from the house to the garden, or getting into the car, or changing from sitting at rest to moving about with purpose, or moving from wakefulness to sleep or vice versa. These are all transitions, and our children may struggle at this granular level as well as with the bigger things. As adults, these may seem insignificant to us and so we may not recognize that our children's behaviour is generated from going through a transition. When we notice that these transitions exist for our children, and that they are finding them hard, we can support them to manage these smaller transitions better and give them life skills that are transferrable to the bigger ones too.

Managing the little transitions

There are lots of diverse ways to handle transitions in daily life. Different situations call for different solutions. Sometimes it is about warning, sometimes about distraction; other times it is about making the change more manageable or simplifying it. Sometimes it is a combination; there is no one size fits all. There are few options here to get you started thinking about things you can do that will suit your child in the situations that you encounter. The more we can help our children manage these little transitions, the more they will be able to regulate themselves and the less confrontation and upset will happen as we go through our day. Managing the little transitions builds skills for managing the big ones too.

Make it clear how long an activity will last: Wherever you can, at the start of an activity, indicate how long it will last. Use language that your child will understand. If the length of the activity is measured in a specific number of turns then count them out so they can tell where they are, or if it is a length of time, use a visual prompt like a timer or the hand on a clock. Give reminders of the progress towards the end of the task to manage their expectations.

Give a five-minute warning: Letting a child know that a transition is coming can help them regulate ahead of the change happening. The classic five-minute warning has its uses in multiple situations. If five minutes is not enough, then do ten- and five-minute warnings. Five and ten are good as they give clear hand gestures to use to signal to your child wherever you are and if they are out of earshot.

Use an object to alert that a change is coming: Creating distance between us and the notification that a change is happening can be helpful to reduce confrontation between ourselves and our child. It is not us telling them to stop, it is the object. A sand timer can be helpful for this. They can be bought for a variety of timescales and are helpful as they show the passage of time as well as the end of the activity and so encourage independence. Technology can help too. Smart speakers can be programmed to make announcements at a set time, and they can even be used to program lights. For example, we programmed ours to count down to when it was time to come off the games console. It announced 15 minutes to go, and the light went green, then ten minutes when the light went blue and in the final five minutes it went red, and the announcement said it was time to save the game. This made it consistent every day and took the pressure off us as we did not need to remember or to keep going through to warn our son that the activity would be ending soon, and it took out any option for negotiation too, as we were not there to plead or argue with.

Make it fun: Introduce games to make the transitions fun, such as getting coats when the floor is lava, blowing bubbles or playing spotting or singing games. Introduce a lightness to what you are doing to distract them and make it less stressful and more enjoyable.

Give choices: Whenever possible, let your child have control over the choices. Give them options to choose from rather than a blank canvas, as this can be overwhelming for them and risky for you as they may choose something that is not available. Let them choose a snack for the journey, for example, or pick the route.

Break it down further: Even a small transition can feel unsettling for a child. Breaking it down into a series of smaller steps can make the transition happen without it being apparent to the child.

For example, a child who loves gardening can become dysregulated when making the change from indoors to outdoors. This may show up in actions like arguing about putting shoes on or stalling behaviours. Splitting the task up makes it more manageable. Perhaps bring some things inside to talk about before going out. Talk about which seeds you are going to plant, choose which pots to put them in, and what tools you will use. Giving them choices makes them feel in control and, as the task has already started, they have transitioned into doing it without realizing. Once it is time to put those wellies on and go out, they are well in the swing so do not feel that a transition is happening.

Acknowledge when they are moving away from something they enjoy: Often we are asking our child to do something that is less engaging for them than the thing they are doing. When a child is being asked to transition from something they love, acknowledging that and showing empathy can help smooth the change. For example, 'I know it is annoying having to stop playing your game. I can see how much further you are getting round the track so you must have been practising hard. I know you would love to keep practising all morning, but we are leaving to meet Aunt Jane now. You can play when we get back before tea.' Ensure that you explain what is happening, give them plenty of warning and make it clear that they can resume their activity later.

Use a transitional object: If your child is going to be apart from you, give them something of yours to take with them or a reminder of you or the family. This can be something of yours or a photo or a favourite object – anything that is familiar and reminds them that they are connected to you.

Make it clear that they are coming back: If you are leaving home, leave something ready for their return; for example, a Lego model that you are working on, a half-finished jigsaw or a story. Or line the cars up ready for a race later. Highlight these to your child to stress that you will be back, and that this is where they belong.

Have journey objects: Have things in your car or in a bag that your child enjoys but only uses during those times. Having things that they want to access can smooth the transition.

Show them that you were thinking of them: If you are away from your child, show them that you missed them on your return. Tell them that you thought of them, take photos of things they would like to share once you are back together. Remind them that even when they cannot see you there is still a connection, and they are in your thoughts.

Have a sensory break: Introduce a sensory activity as part of the transition, such as bouncing on a trampoline, doing star jumps, hopping or skipping. Use a fidget toy, resistance bands or play putty – anything that initiates heavy work to calm the sensory system.

Fill the dead space: Sometimes in between activities there can be periods of waiting. These can be tough for children to manage and can create problems down the line as you transition into the next thing. Make use of these to help your children to regulate. Do an activity together. Have a game or a book with you or use an app on your phone. Something as simple as using filters on a phone can pass the time and build connection. Or have a movement break to use up restless energy and aid regulation. My son used to love being timed running so we could often be found outside a restaurant between courses with him doing sprints while I congratulated him on his ever-decreasing time. Doing something in this time makes these moments a positive experience for you all and that positivity feeds into the transition and the next activity too.

Allow time: If you know a transition is going to be tough, build in plenty of time to achieve it. Feeling rushed builds tensions and makes things worse, so feeling as if we have plenty of time helps us to stay calm and our children stay calm too.

Recognize when a transition goes well and praise your child for this. There will be lots of these during the day, but we can miss them and instead only notice when it goes wrong. Mention it when they put the iPad down without complaint, when they get ready for school seamlessly. Be enthusiastic and reward these moments and you will see more of them.

Meeting someone new

Meeting someone new can be a daunting experience for anyone. Help your child by making the person known to them ahead of the actual meeting. If it is a friend or another child, share stories about them or pictures, share anything you know about them that would pique your child's interest. If it is a professional, get as much information as you can and ideally ask them for some facts and a photo ahead of the meeting to make them seem more familiar.

Going somewhere new

When you are visiting an unfamiliar place, give your child as much information as you can ahead of time. Use Google Street View to travel the route and view the area. If it is a public place, they may have information available on their website, including pictures, or some places have interactive online tours too. If it is a venue that is geared for children visiting, they may have additional resources such as visual stories to introduce the building and what they do. These can often be found as part of their accessibility or autism-friendly resources; however, they are applicable to support any children who may find going somewhere new difficult.

Managing the big transitions

Some transitions can be anticipated and give us the opportunity to lay the groundwork to make things as smooth as possible. Coping with a transition takes time and repetition. The more familiarity we can build in, the more confident our child will feel.

Well ahead of the change happening, talk through it with your child, listen to any worries they may have and help them to talk about the emotions they may be feeling. Create a visual calendar to enable them to see the passing of time as we move towards the change. Check with your child if they want it somewhere that they can see it as they may not want a constant reminder that change is coming. Use books that deal with this change as a starting point for conversations. Talk to other parents and children who may have done this previously for tips and insider information. Ideally visit so they get to know the location, but where this is not an option show your child pictures. Give them as much information as you can and ensure there is an open dialogue to enable them to ask questions and voice concerns. Remind them of other things like this they have done in the past. Build on previous success and learning. Where you can, give them opportunities to have some control. For a new school year, that could be choosing a schoolbag or pencil case, for a house move it could be choosing how to decorate their bedroom. Anything that helps them feel they have some choice. Create as much familiarity as possible to help your child know what to expect.

During a time of transition, remember that under stress we regress. Your child may display behaviours that they have not done for a while, or some behaviours may become more pronounced. Change wobbles us. To help maintain a sense of stability, ensure that anything that can stay the same does. Keep your routines and family traditions going to create certainty around the uncertainty. Do everything you can to maintain connection with your child. Give them transitional objects, things that smell of you, or little notes in their lunch box or pockets. We had little keyring photos of us as a family on our kids' schoolbags for example, to remind them that they belonged and were loved even though we were not with them at that moment. Play games together, do the things you both enjoy, remind them that although some things have changed in their life, you are still there, and your love and presence are constant.

High days and holidays

Children who thrive on structure and routine can find days where things are different or there is less structure incredibly challenging and unsettling; for example, days like birthdays where there is a lot of excitement and energy, or Christmas where layer upon layer of overwhelm can make functioning difficult. Managing these special days and the days when they are off school on holiday or we are away somewhere different can be challenging for them and for us, but there are some things we can do to dial the emotion down and make these days more enjoyable for everyone.

Anniversaries

The anniversary of when a child joins a family can be a triggering time. It can remind them and us of those early days and can bring uncertainty and break connection. Children who are hypervigilant will find cues that we may never notice to alert them that an anniversary is coming, and this can lead to them feeling wobbled and they may regress or act out. Being aware that this could happen, and recognizing it when it does, can help us to support our child and to put things in place to lessen the impact in future years. Support your child by helping them to see what lies beneath these feelings and behaviours and talk openly and empathetically with them about this. Do as many activities as you can to build connection both in the small things you do and the bigger things.

Birthdays

Many children find their birthday a day where things can become too much. All that waiting, the presents, the party, being the centre of attention, plus the additional sugar consumption, can be a recipe for overwhelm.

Make sure that your child knows what will be happening on the day ahead of time. Create a visual timetable to help them to know what to expect and when. Keep it low key and fit it around your child.

If your child finds presents difficult, keep the number for them to open to a minimum. If it helps, tell them what they are getting ahead of time. That is hard for us, as we want to have that element of surprise on the day, but it can be what our children need to manage the day successfully.

For some children, a big party may not be something that they will find manageable, so if that is the case then find something lower key to do. We had one year with just close family and another with just two or three kids at the house doing a planned activity which gave them focus but still gave the sense of a birthday celebration.

Plan their birthday around what will work for them, not on what society or friends or family members think it should be. After all, it's their party!

Christmas

The build up to Christmas is relentless and for many children can be completely overwhelming. All routine at school goes out of the window on the run up to the Christmas holidays. There are nativity and school show rehearsals, parties, concerts and everywhere they look a sensory overload of trees, decorations and lights. At home, the house looks different with the decorations up, different foods appear, and Mum and Dad are more stressed than ever. I am not sure that sounds like the most wonderful time of the year to me!

Much of this is not in our control, but some things are. Think about what happens on the run up to Christmas and where possible keep your routines in place so your children have as much structure as possible in their lives. Build in connection-giving activities to help your child to regulate and feel connected to you and the family. Keep it low key as much as you can. Do not add in extra activities if your child is already overstretched with what they are doing at school. Keep checking in with your child and be prepared to drop out of things at the last moment if they will not manage.

Be flexible, take things as they come and be in tune with your child and what they can cope with. You are the expert on your child, and you will know best what will work for them.

On Christmas Day, organize things in a way that will support your child to regulate and enjoy the day. If they are worried about Santa coming into the house, explain that you have talked to the big chap about leaving the gifts in the garage or a shed. Create a visual schedule of the day so they know what to expect and when. Make sure that there is space in it for your child to be able to decompress. Perhaps build in a walk or something that will burn off some excess energy. If necessary, open some, or all, of the presents on Christmas Eve to take the pressure off on Christmas Day when there may be family around. Build Christmas Day around what will suit your family, not around what convention says it should be.

School holidays

The school holidays, in particular the summer, can feel endless for parents and for children. Helping our children to remain regulated when the structure of the school week is not present is challenging. Where possible, add structure. The structure may vary from week to week but ensure that your child is aware of what is happening and when. Stick to your daily routine as much as you can. It is tempting to become less rigid when school is out, but our children need the predictability that a routine brings, and it will help them to feel safe and secure. It also makes it easier at the end of the holiday as you do not need to get back into a routine if you are still in it. Build in a bit of space for you if you can; school holidays are challenging for parents as well as children.

Going away on holiday

Going away on holiday is a wonderful thing and creates memories that the whole family will remember for many years to come. Holidays are full of new experiences, new locations and new people. Going away is magical but can be stressful too. Ahead of time, familiarize your child with the location you are going to. Look at photos, videos, read reviews on Trip Advisor. Create a countdown to the holiday and a vision board of images to remind them of where they are going and what it will be like. Use Google Street View to look around the destination, find the places you might go and things you may see. Perhaps create a schedule of the journey so they know what transport they will be on and how long each step will take. Involve them in making a list, choosing their holiday clothes and packing the case to encourage them to feel part of things and to be familiar with what they are taking too. While you are away, ensure that as much of the routine as possible still exists. Still have your bedtime routine, for example. It might happen later, but the structure can be the same. The more things you can retain that are familiar, the more your child will feel safe and secure and able to enjoy the trip.

Chapter 5

UNDERSTANDING BEHAVIOUR

Can you remember some occasions when you talked about a shared experience with a friend and disagreed about what happened? Or can you think of an occasion when you had a remarkably similar experience to a friend but you both reacted differently? Or a time when your child reacted in a way that did not make sense to you?

Perception and reality

We each operate under the misapprehension that how we experience the world is the same as others do. We believe that our memories are exact internal representations of the external world. However, the reality is far from this. In fact, we all process the world in our own way and none of us will react to an experience in the same way as someone else. At every moment, we are unconsciously choosing what we notice. Every second, our five senses send two million pieces of information to our brain. Our conscious mind can process fewer than 200 pieces of information per second, so our brains are discarding more than 99.99 per cent of the information available to us. Selecting the pieces of information that we need from this deluge is like trying to drink from a fire hose. The selections our brains unconsciously make are based on our memories and our life experiences. Our history informs how we decide whether our actions are good or bad, right or wrong, and how we feel about ourselves, others and the world. Our past creates our current values, beliefs and attitudes.

The decisions on which pieces of information to keep and which to discard are done in a split second without our conscious awareness. Our brains filter the information automatically. All this filtering happens at a subconscious level. It is like changing gear in a car. When you first learned to drive, it was a very thought-intensive process, but in time it became second nature. Our filtering has developed like this, becoming increasingly automatic over the years until it has become invisible. The information our brain actively chooses to pay attention to creates our very own worldview, our internal representation of the world. Two people can represent an identical external experience in a vastly different way internally.

The life experiences that our children have experienced will have shaped their internal processing. They will interpret the world based on the perceptions they have developed. Their early life experiences may have shaped their brains to look for danger, to focus on the negative and so that is all they will see. Everything else will not make it past their filters. It will be as if it does not exist.

The good news is that these patterns can change. Our brains (and our children's brains) are adaptable. We can change what happens unconsciously by changing what we focus on consciously.

One thing leads to another

As we have seen, our perception of the world is not reality, it is a tiny subset of reality chosen based on the sum of our experiences throughout our growth and development as human beings. Our perception of the world and of ourselves shapes our thoughts, feelings and behaviours. Our thoughts, feelings and behaviours are all linked together. Our thoughts change how we feel, which then alters how we act, which then influences our thoughts, and round and round it goes.

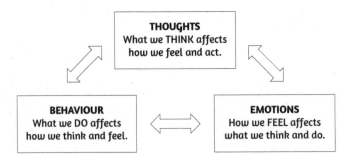

So how does this work in practice? Let us think about the morning of a stressed, tired parent who is getting their kids to school. The parent gets the children up. As the children are getting dressed some squabbling starts. The parent starts thinking that their children do not listen, that things are going to go wrong. They start feeling tired and stressed and irritated, so they start to talk loudly; then they get cross and tell the kids off. Then they wish they hadn't done that, and think that they are a terrible parent. They feel guilty and exhausted. They bundle the kids into the car to get to school and as soon as the kids leave, they sit slumped at the steering wheel thinking about how they can't cope, and feeling overwhelmed.

Sound familiar? I know I have been (and sometimes still am) that parent. My thoughts feed negative emotions, which feed behaviours I don't like, leading to even more negative thoughts and emotions. It's a vicious spiral heading downwards.

Changing our minds

As we have seen, the reality that we experience is largely determined by what we do inside our heads. Some things are within our control and other things are outside our control. One of the things that we do have agency over are our thoughts. Some of the stress we feel is generated by the power of our mind. When we are stressed and feeling overwhelmed, although we may not realize it, the negative thoughts that we generate about ourselves can be a permanent undermining force. These thoughts can be hideously vindictive, swirling through our minds without us noticing, bringing with them a wave of emotion and self-doubt. In the example of the stressed, tired parent we saw earlier, what if instead of noticing what the children were doing wrong, they noticed what they were doing right? And what if they changed the narrative in their head to be more supporting? Might the morning have gone differently? Let's look...

As the children are getting dressed some squabbling starts. Instead of thinking that that their children do not listen, that things are going to go wrong, the parent instead notices how quickly the children have got dressed. Ignoring the squabbling, they all go down for breakfast. More squabbling breaks out. The parent thinks they all seem quite anxious as mornings are always a little stressful, and that a singalong in the car might help everyone relax a bit before school. They have fun together and the kids leave the car ready to start a day at school.

How we think affects how we feel and how we behave. In tandem with our filters, which select what we see in the world, this creates our reality.

Being aware of our thoughts and our filters gives us the ability to change them – to challenge the thoughts that don't serve us well, and to change our filters to see a better world that was there all the time.

Noticing negative thoughts and patterns that we and our children are falling into enables us to acknowledge that these thoughts are there and bring them out of the subconscious gloom that they currently inhabit and into conscious awareness. When we notice them, we recognize them for the imposters they are.

Here are some examples of negative thoughts:

- I can't cope, I'm weak and stupid.
- I made a mistake; I am a failure.
- It was not good enough, everything is ruined.
- She is so much better than me.
- I never learn.
- It is all going to go wrong.
- He never listens to me.
- She does not like me.
- He is late because he does not care.
- It is all my fault.
- I have messed up; I knew I would.
- I am not a good parent.

So, when you feel your mood is affected, or you notice that you are thinking negatively about yourself or your family, focus your attention on what you are thinking and feeling.

About the thought: Is the thought true? Would someone else agree? Would you speak like that to a friend? Would a friend speak to you like that? Forgive yourself. Accept that we all make mistakes.

About the feeling: How are you feeling? What name would you give the emotion (e.g. anger, sadness, exhaustion, despair)? Don't be tempted to skip naming the emotion, as this is essential to controlling how you feel about the thought. Magnetic resonance imaging (MRI) studies of the brain have found that two things happen when you label a negative emotion: activity in your amygdala (your primitive fear centre) goes down, while activity in your prefrontal cortex (the centre of organized thought) goes up. So, naming the emotion removes its primitive power and moves your thoughts into a more rational sphere of consciousness.

Believe in yourself and your ability to cope. Catch those passing thoughts and challenge them. Our obedient brains look for more of the things we direct them towards, so the more we see ourselves and our families positively, the more positivity we will see around us. And like a snowball rolling down a hill, it will quickly gain momentum and grow all by itself.

Raising a child with developmental trauma is tough. When we do it well, we often get harsh judgements and eyebrow raises from family, friends and even strangers. Most people just don't get it. Our children have different needs from many of their peers and so require a different kind of parenting. Good parenting isn't seen in the behaviour of the child, but in the behaviour of the parent.

We often carry tremendous guilt; guilt for the things that were done to our child before we even met them, guilt for times when we feel we got it wrong, guilt for not doing enough or doing too much. Our children can present differently outside the home, so our lived experience is often doubted. Our children can be expert manipulators, controlling, hypervigilant and anxious. They can have emotional needs that are beyond the capacity of one human being to meet. We love our children even when they reject us; we hope and we love, and no matter how tired we are we get up the next day and do it all again. Occasionally we get a glimpse of the child they would have been had they been untouched by trauma, and although the vision is fleeting and heartbreaking, it fuels us to redouble our efforts in the hope of seeing more of that wonderful inner child.

When things are tough, we can fear our own inability to cope and it can become a self-fulfilling prophecy where we worry about our capabilities, fill our minds with derogatory self-talk, and focus on the negative. If we do not achieve what we set out to do, or if things go wrong, then this proves our original fears, causing our confidence to plummet still further. Giving ourselves credit is fundamental in breaking this cycle. Be aware of any tendency to focus only on the negatives, and look for the positives within yourself and in your interactions with others.

The end of a day is often a time for reflection and sometimes it can be easy to dwell on what went wrong in the day, rather than what went right. Remembering bad things gives us a negative opinion of the day and of ourselves. Remembering good things reframes our day as positive and boosts self-belief. Finish each day thinking about what went well, about what you achieved, about moments of attachment. Set a positive intention for the next day; it doesn't have to be something big, make it as small as you like. Make sure it is achievable, and when you do it, celebrate your success.

Exploring emotions

As we have seen, our thoughts, emotions and behaviour are all linked. How our children behave is shaped by their underlying thoughts and emotions. Adults often focus on the behaviour because this is the part they can see. However, like an iceberg, only a tiny part of what is going on for our children is visible. Underneath the surface behaviour, hidden from sight, are their thoughts and feelings – their need to belong, to feel safe; their lack of understanding due to limited social skills or poor executive function; their internal body responses; their sensory overwhelm; their underlying emotions of fear, anger, sadness or guilt and shame.

If their behaviour seems off, then the chances are that they are feeling off. Something is going on inside that is leading to the behaviour. One of the most important things we can teach our children is that feelings are okay, that there is nothing they can say or do that would make us love them less. We support our children's healthy emotional development every time we respond to their difficult thoughts and feelings by accepting them and expressing empathy.

Understanding what lies beneath behaviours helps us to understand our children and ourselves better. When we understand, we are more able to accept and nurture our child and support them to understand and accept themselves.

All behaviour is communication

Much of what is perceived to be misbehaviour is the expression of a child's unmet emotional needs and consequently their low sense of self-worth. The child isn't choosing to behave in this way. In the moment, they are unable to behave in another way. At such times, reasoning, demanding or bribing does nothing to address their unmet need, but using empathy goes a long way to helping them to turn things around.

Showing empathy

Empathy is the ability to step into another person's shoes, understand what they are feeling and see things from their perspective. With empathy, you seek to imagine or understand how someone feels, without necessarily having those feelings yourself. As parents, it can be hard to avoid the powerful urge to fix things for our children, to give advice, to assume that what we would feel is what they do feel. Difficult feelings can't just be fixed; however, when they are listened to, accepted and understood, the feelings become much less difficult, and by showing empathy we allow our child to feel calmer and more secure.

In our family, we learned how powerful empathy can be in the first year after we adopted our son. At this time, our daughter would sometimes get very distressed and express how she didn't want him to be there and how he had stolen her life. Initially, I tried reasoning with her, talking about how she had been in favour of the adoption process. Her response was that she had been, but she wished we had adopted anyone but him. I would continue trying to reason with her, highlighting his good points, what she had gained by having a younger brother. Her distress made me feel upset and guilty, so I was trying to fix it, to make it go away. I could see that what I was doing was not helping either of us. I realized that I was arguing with her about how she felt, not hearing her point of view and trying to persuade her to feel differently. My intentions were good, but I was making her feel worse. So, the next time she got upset about it, instead of negating her feelings, I empathized with how she felt. I accepted her feelings and her reality. I said that I could see how hard this was for her and how it must be tough feeling so distressed. We had a long chat and ended up cuddled together on her bed. The outcome when I empathized was totally different from the outcome that had happened before. She felt heard, she felt understood and accepted, and together we felt a strong connection.

Some things to think of when showing empathy:

Give them space to process and say things in their own time: We all process things at different speeds. Allow your child thinking time and sit with them quietly while they think.

Acknowledge their feelings: Show that you have heard what they have said, that you are there for them and that it's okay to feel that way.

Wonder about the name of the feeling: Often a child will not know what the feeling is. We can try to imagine what it may be like from their point of view and offer our guesses as to how they are feeling. Try to suggest what it might be by saying things like, 'I wonder if you are feeling...?' or, 'I think if that had happened to me, I might be feeling... Is that the same for you?' or, 'You look a bit sad today. Has anything happened?' Don't worry about getting it wrong. They will still feel heard and will sense that you are being authentic and that could be just the opening that they need to name the feeling for themselves.

To help you get started, here are a few possible emotions to use: glad, pleased, happy, playful, cheerful, calm, comfortable, cosy, safe, relaxed, confident, peaceful, curious, excited, bubbly, silly, thankful, loved, loving, satisfied, proud, wonderful, delighted, sad, unhappy, gloomy, annoyed, mean, grumpy, grouchy, uncomfortable, startled, scared, anxious, worried, shy, nervous, weird, confused, quiet, jealous, embarrassed, guilty, responsible, unfair, ashamed, bored, disappointed, hurt, lost, sorry, lonely, discouraged, awful, disgusted, mad, angry, frustrated, impatient, threatened, afraid, shaky, miserable, horrified.

Be interested and ask questions about their feelings: When does it happen? Where do they feel it in their body? Does it have a shape? A colour? A sound? Is it heavy? Or light? Is it hot? Or cold? Does it vibrate? Or move around?

Thank them for sharing and having the courage to open up: It's a big thing to share feelings and we want to encourage our children to feel able to do it readily. Tell them that you are there for them, that you accept and love them unconditionally and always will. Offer to be with them, to have a cuddle, to just be together without talking if that is what they need in the moment. You can talk about things later when they are more able to.

Often a solution won't be needed, but if it is, help them to find it themselves by encouraging them to think about options.

Talking about feelings

Be open to talking about all kinds of feelings, positive and negative. Avoid doing it in the heat of the moment where emotions are heightened. Wait to have the meaningful conversation when you are both calm. Talking things through helps your child to develop a vocabulary around their feelings and to know that it is okay to share them. Talk to them about what gives them joy and what they love, and talk about things that have made them angry or afraid too. Your child's brain is still developing, they are learning to handle their emotions and communicate clearly, so the more you help them to talk about emotions, the better they will understand them and be able to handle them.

Build reflecting positive and negative emotions into your everyday interactions. The more you do it in the little moments the more your children will be comfortable in the big ones.

- You look so comfortable and cosy on the sofa, how lovely.
- That cake looks delicious, I can see you are really enjoying it.
- Wow, you've built an enormous tower, you look proud of it. Well done you, great balancing.
- It sounds like you are feeling a bit sorry for yourself, do you want a cuddle?
- You look very pleased with yourself.
- Are you curious to see what is under the stone? Do you feel a little nervous? Or excited maybe?
- That sounds disappointing, it's hurtful when we work hard at something and someone doesn't like it.

Sometimes when you start to show empathy it can seem to lead to an increase in the intensity of your child's expressions of their feelings. This can feel worrying but is a positive sign as it shows that they are starting to feel safe enough to experience and express their emotions.

Recognizing that feelings and behaviour are linked

Understanding that behaviour is driven by big feelings inside helps us and our children address the underlying causes and see that they are often not in control of their behaviour. When we ask questions in an open and accepting way, we enable our children to think about their behaviours in a way that is curious, that focuses on learning and avoids blame and the consequent shame.

When an incident happens that you want to talk about with your child, it is helpful to have a clear process that you go through with them that they and you understand. We had a pictogram chart that we used that helped us to think things through together. We used it when something had happened at school and we also shared it with school, and they used it too so that there was consistency in approach.

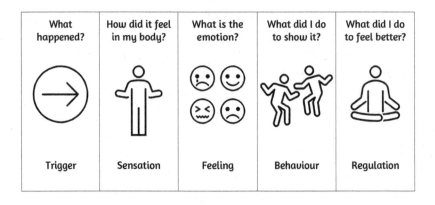

What happened?	How did it feel in my body?	What is the emotion?	What did I do to show it?	What did I do to feel better?
Trigger	Sensation	Feeling	Behaviour	Regulation

This type of pictogram gives a structure to talk through what happened, what the sensations were in their body, what the feeling was and what the resulting behaviour was, finishing on a positive of how they managed the emotion and calmed down. Ask questions in a calm and curious way and help your child to see how they could do things differently another time. Focus on the opportunity to learn. Perhaps they could avoid the trigger or recognize the feeling and do something earlier on to calm down. The more we talk through behaviours and the underlying causes, the better our child can understand and do something different another time. It can take lots of repetition; it's hard to manage emotions and, for our children, there can be triggers everywhere. However, when we talk things through in a calm and accepting way with them, they feel loved and connected and are more able to learn and adapt.

Wondering

A child who has experienced trauma in their early life will often struggle to verbalize their emotions. Wondering is a powerful tool to enable children to become more self-aware and learn to regulate their internal states. When you notice a change in your child's behaviour, describe what you see to them and wonder aloud what it might mean. For example, 'I noticed you touching your neck as we got out of the car. I wonder if you are feeling a little anxious about going to cubs tonight?' or, 'Your face was beaming when you came out of school today. I wonder what happened to make you look so happy and proud?'

Practising seeing things from another point of view

Showing empathy to our children will encourage them to show it too. Encourage them to practise by talking about what others are feeling when reading books or watching TV. Ask questions about how the other people might be feeling or thinking. Ask open questions like, 'What do you think he is feeling?' or, 'What do you think he is thinking?' or, 'What would you do if you were him?' or, 'How would you solve the problem?'

When they are telling you about their day, talk about another person's viewpoint. Ask simple questions such as, 'How do you think Amy felt when everyone clapped?' or, 'I wonder how John felt when everyone laughed?' or, 'What do you think the teacher was feeling when you were all shouting and not paying attention?' Help them to reflect about the other person's feelings. For a younger child, you may need to help them by making suggestions. Being curious about others helps our children to feel comfortable talking about feelings and practise seeing things from another person's point of view.

Help your child to see the similarities between themselves and others – their classmates, family members, characters in a book or on TV, people who are older, or younger, in other countries and cultures. Help them to feel connected with the world around them.

Expressing empathy and encouraging our children to show empathy leads to greater emotional intelligence and resilience. At first it may feel a little strange to you and to them but persevere. It will not only help your child to feel heard and understood but will equip them with a language and understanding of their feelings, and the feelings of those around them, for life. It enables them to feel safe enough to show their true feelings without fear of rejection. When we show interest in hearing and understanding our children's feelings, it increases the bond between us, and our children will feel unconditionally loved and accepted.

Narrating your internal experience

Narrating what we are feeling and thinking can help our children understand what is happening in our internal world and how we manage our emotions, which in turn helps them understand and manage themselves. It helps them to see that others can feel big emotions, that they aren't alone. Talk about the positive as well as the negative. For example, 'Sitting on the sofa with you is giving me a warm, cosy feeling. I can feel my shoulders have dropped and I feel so relaxed. This is lovely. I like it when we cuddle up together' or, 'When I was speaking to Jane earlier on, I could feel I was getting hot, and that anxious butterflies feeling was happening in my tummy. I took a few big breaths and reminded myself that I could do it and I felt calmer and able to carry on talking.'

Sometimes we all feel overwhelmed and need space. If that is the case, explain what is happening and why to your child so they understand, and it doesn't get stressful for them. For example, 'I am going into the garden to do some star jumps to calm down because I am getting that burning feeling in my chest which means I know I am getting cross, and I don't want to get shouty.' This way we show how we regulate and we model it for them at the same time as regulating ourselves. When we aren't regulated, we can't help our child regulate. Being open about our feelings and managing them enables us to co-regulate with our children.

Shaping your response to show them what they need

Secure attachments grow from a caregiver consistently and appropriately being responsive to a child's needs. Where a child is unable to give these cues, as parents we can shape our responses to help the child to learn what the need is. For example, if they have hurt themselves, comfort them even if they do not appear upset. Verbalize what they may be feeling. Do the same when you are experiencing an internal feeling – say out loud when you are hurt, or hungry. Show pleasure when you see them, talk about positive and negative emotions. Help your child to see when the same might be true for them. Give them the words to talk about what they feel so they can let the emotions out. When we as adults respond to a child's emotions, they learn that these can be shared. When a child has their emotions ignored or suppressed, then they learn to handle these for themselves, leading to feelings of fear and confusion.

Identifying the underlying need

Sometimes children will talk in ways that adults can perceive as rude or demanding. Children who experience inconsistency or lack of safety in their early lives can have an inability to express their feelings and may also have a need to control in order to feel safe. So, how do we handle it when our children speak in ways that we may find challenging, or that others may react negatively to? They may say things like 'Give me some food' or, 'Pick me up' or, 'Go away'. They may be doing it in a clumsy way, but they are expressing a real need and there is a positive intention behind their words. When an unwelcome behaviour is directed at us, this can help us to detach, and stop us from taking things personally. They are telling us that they are hungry, that they feel unsafe, or that they are having trouble regulating themselves. Help them by meeting the need that is behind the demand. For example, 'It sounds as if you are hungry; there is a yogurt in the fridge' or, 'It sounds as if you are feeling a bit worried; do you want a cuddle?' or, 'I can see that you want to be on your own. That's fine, I will be over here any time you want to join me.'

Rethinking power and control

Babies are born programmed to seek out the things they need to survive, to meet their physical, psychological, and emotional needs. Most parents of newborns shape their day around the baby, sleeping when the baby sleeps, snatching food and leaving half-drunk cups of tea around. Effectively, the baby controls the adults although we do not see this as controlling; instead we understand that babies are dependent on us, and their needs must be satisfied. When the baby's needs are met in a predictable way, as the baby grows and develops into childhood they have less and less need to control the adults and become increasingly able to meet their own needs.

Where a child does not have their needs met in a predictable way as a baby, they may have unconsciously learned to respond in a particular way to get their fundamental survival needs met. This becomes a pattern that they continue because it is how they have learned that they must be to have their needs met.

This can lead to them becoming controlling of the environment and people around them. This can be seen in children dominating play with others, or attempts to parent peers or even adults, and resisting parental boundaries and limits. When their control is questioned, they can find this extremely distressing as they unconsciously believe that the control is what is keeping them safe.

When you observe controlling behaviour in your child, think about how you would response to a much younger child, to a one-year-old for example. Remain calm and allow them as much control as you can, and remember that they are behaving in this way to feel safe. When a child feels that they have power with the adults as well as power over themselves, they will learn that they do not need to seek power over others.

Ways to help your child meet their power needs

Power is not like a torch where only one person can have it at a time. There is not a finite amount of power, so giving some to our child makes no difference to how much we have. Power is more like a candle flame – where when we share it, it grows, and we do not lose any of what we already had. Our children are not trying to take our power, they are seeking power of their own.

Offer choice: Giving them more choices could be letting them pick out their clothing, what they have in their lunch box, what story they get at bedtime – anything where you can give them autonomy over what happens.

Foster independence: Give them some responsibilities at home. These do not have to be big things; little things are just as effective and can be more age appropriate. For example, jobs like picking up leaves in the garden, watering the plants, emptying the dishwasher, putting their dirty laundry in the washing basket, helping with the grocery shopping, and putting the groceries away. Having responsibility fosters independence.

Ask their opinion: Include them in decisions where you can. Ask them for their input into small and large choices; daily choices like what to have for tea, or big ones like where to go on holiday. Make them feel that they have a voice and their opinion matters.

Ask for their help: Asking our children to help us makes them feel valued. They can help with food preparation and cooking, sorting laundry, hanging out laundry, gardening or cleaning. There are lots of jobs around the home that, when they do them with you, give them a sense of being grown up and useful and that build skills for later life.

Obey the rules not the adults: Having clearly defined family rules means that the boundaries are clear and both parties understand them. This means that when your child breaks a rule, you can point out that they broke a rule. This avoids the 'do what I say' narrative which leads to destructive power struggles – and there are no winners in a power struggle.

Respect their boundaries: Knock on their bedroom door before entering, ask if they want a cuddle, allow them to say no to things. If Auntie Mary grabs them for a sloppy kiss and they do not want it, intervene. They have a right to personal space, so show them that it is okay to say no. Behaving in this way teaches our child to respect themselves and plants the seeds of consent and boundaries that others should respect about their body at an early age.

Learning to make choices and be independent is an important part of growing up. When we give our child freedom and responsibility, they take ownership and feel empowered.

A child seeking to control is not power-hungry, they are safety-hungry. They are communicating a need. When we see the child and their behaviour differently, we see a different child.

Thinking about thinking

When you look around you at this moment, what do you see? Think of three things that are good about this experience. Now think of three things that are bad about this experience.

What you saw was the same in both cases, but the way you thought about it was different. The reality was the same, but your perception changed. This is a simple example, but all experiences in life can be looked at in multiple ways. There is always a choice on where we put our focus. So where do we put our focus on our children? Do we notice more good? Or more bad?

In the hurly burly of family life, it can be all too easy to get stuck in a pattern of noticing the things that our children cannot do, or did not do, rather than what they can or did do. When we do this, we build up filters that selectively notice all behaviour that supports this rather than any evidence to the contrary. Their negative behaviour becomes what we notice and the positive things that they do get filtered out. In effect, we just do not see the positive.

If we only notice the negative, and comment on it, we build a pattern in our children where they too recognize the negative in themselves and miss the positive. It is hard to feel good about yourself if you are surrounded by evidence to the contrary.

One of the most powerful ways we can interrupt these unconscious processes is to change our focus and turn our attention to notice when we are thinking negatively about our children and at the same time focus on new and positive things. In doing so, we change our filters and change how we see our children, which changes our behaviour towards them, which changes how they see themselves.

Look for positive actions and intent in your child's behaviour. Each time you see them doing something good or trying to do something good, notice it. Think to yourself 'that was good' and focus on what it was that they did that was good. Think about it in positive language. If you notice yourself thinking of negative things, look for the positive intent from the child, or their point of view. Dumping a coat on the ground could be because they are excited to be home for example.

The human brain is an incredible success machine. Whatever we program it to look for, it will find. Teach it to look for failure in our children and it will home in on that. Teach it to look for success and that is what it will find. It is very accommodating. What we tell our mind is what we get. The good news is that we can control what we focus on and so change what our mind is looking for.

Changing your focus to the positive can adjust the filters to let in the positive and leave the negative behind. When we bring the same degree of forensic attention to when things go well as we do to when they go badly – when we notice the positive in our children – they will too.

Accepting them and loving them just as they are

All children are different; they each have their own unique strengths and weaknesses. They vary physically, intellectually, socially and emotionally. We need to match our expectations to what they can do. What one child finds easy will be a struggle for another; some children pick new things up quickly, others take longer. If we expect too much or too little of our children, they can become rebellious, frustrated or angry, and the pressure can lead to them giving up and feeling a failure, which will impact on their confidence.

If we want our children to grow up mentally secure and confident then we need to listen to them, to take the time to really notice the changes in what they can do, comparing it to what they could do yesterday or last week. Do not compare it to what others are achieving, what their siblings achieved, or to what you might think that they 'should' be able to do – this is about *them*, about celebrating their progress against a benchmark of themselves, no one else. It is about being the best they can be, which is not necessarily the best in comparison to others. Maybe today they managed to tie their shoelaces which they did not manage last week, or they did their homework (or part of it) unaided.

Focus on individual tasks and recognize each small step in their learning. Each of these individual steps are a movement towards a greater goal. The only way to reach any destination is one step at a time and it is vital for children to learn that we see and celebrate each step of progress rather than just when a large milestone is reached. Over time, this pattern will lead them to recognize and celebrate their own small successes as well as the big ones, which will give them pride in themselves and their achievements.

So, think about what your child can do and set your expectations at their level. By doing this, your child will feel nurtured and accepted and they will also recognize their own achievements for the milestones that they are, which will boost their self-esteem.

When you notice them doing something good, tell them. Be specific. What is good about it? Is it the time they spent, the effort they put in? Is it how kind they were, how it made the other person feel? Is it better than last time? Is it just lovely to look at? Nice colours? Great attention to detail or focus?

When they want to show you something, or tell you something, STOP and think about what the most important thing is in that moment. Is it the task that you are doing? Or is it building and maintaining a strong and loving relationship with your child? These moments are the cornerstones of parenting. Sometimes you will not be able to stop, so in these cases, find a way to ask them to tell you later that shows that you want to know but it just cannot be now. And all the other times (which should be many more than the other) stop and listen, be truly present, look for positives and give them your time and your attention.

Finding strengths

As parents, because we want to be there for our children, it can be easy to slip into a habit of focusing on things our child needs help and support with, or how to make things better. We do need to notice where we need to put scaffolding up and where we can solve problems, but focusing on weakness can be demoralizing for our children and for us too and can take our attention away from their strengths. Our child's strengths and interests will form the foundation of their future life, and focusing on these and cultivating them will build self-esteem in our child and a sense of pride in us.

Think about things like attention to detail, kindness, honesty, being helpful, loyal, working hard, being creative, patient, enthusiastic, having problem-solving skills, visualization, curiosity, powers of observation, optimism, energy, listening skills, generosity, independence, imagination, academic skills, sporting skills, musical and artistic skills. Their strengths are the things they are good at or have the potential to be good at and that they enjoy doing.

Observe your child and think about what strengths you are seeing. What do they enjoy? What do they have a natural aptitude for? What do they seek out? Think about hidden strengths. For example, hypervigilant children can be great at finding things and directions. Gather information from teachers, other parents, and family members. Talk to your child about it too to see where they think their strengths are.

Once you have identified some strengths, highlight them regularly to your child and encourage activities that play to their strengths. When they do well at something, be specific about the strengths they are exhibiting. If they have a passion, lean into it, take pictures or videos of them doing it and share these regularly with them. When we identify and nurture our child's strengths, we enable them to believe in themselves and reach their potential.

Changing your child's mind

We have already started to change our focus to the positive about our children, but they too may be stuck in a cycle of negative focus about themselves. They may be constantly noticing the negative and discounting the positive.

Having things around you that remind you of your success, great times and those who love you does a power of good for your self-image. It is hard to think badly of yourself when surrounded by evidence to the contrary. So how do we surround our children with positivity? Remind them of their positive qualities and encourage them to look for the positive in themselves and others.

A wonderful wall: In your child's room, create a display of positive feedback items. Include things like certificates and medals, photos of them having fun, photos of their friends and family, phrases from teachers or others praising them, writing and pictures they have done which they are proud of; anything that makes them feel good about themselves. Talk about the items on the wall regularly with your child, reinforce the positive. Revisit it periodically, keep it fresh and relevant.

A memory bank: Children are very visual, and love to look at pictures and physical representations of things that they have made or experienced. It is all too easy to forget past achievements or lose sight of who we are and what we can do. Create a physical resource that your children can go to and remember past successes and enjoyable occasions. This gives them a memory bank of positive resources which they can dip into any time they need to make a withdrawal to top up their reserves of positivity. They can keep adding to it, so over time you will create a wonderful resource together to remind your child of special times and how valued and loved they are.

A feel-good book: It is a lovely idea to get your child to decorate a personal scrapbook, a 'feel-good book' for them to record their positive notes so they can look at them whenever they wish and remember good things they have been praised for. It is fun to also include memories of days out, including photos, or tickets collected and stuck onto paper or made into a collage. It does not have to be a work of art; all it needs is a glue stick or some sticky tape and a sheet of A4.

Three stars and a wish: Encourage your child to take some time each day at bedtime to think of three things they did well that day – their three stars. These do not have to be big. Small things work well. It could be a conversation, something they are proud of, an accomplishment or a time when they helped someone. For example, 'I noticed that someone was sad and went to talk to them' or, 'I had fun playing with John, I shared well' or, 'I told a funny joke that made Mummy smile'. The important thing is to help them focus on accomplishments. When we help our children to expect success, look for success and celebrate success, they find more success and gain more confidence. Of course, they need to learn from their mistakes, but let us help them not to dwell on them. Once they have their three stars, then get them to think of something they plan to do tomorrow to make the day more positive. Their wish. For example: 'I am going to help Anna with her maths' or, 'I am going to say something kind to Miss Smith' or, 'I am going to do a puzzle with my brother after school'. It can be helpful to record these in a journal, and it can be fun to do your own three stars and a wish along with them.

Positive affirmations: Think about positive attributes with your child and create affirmations; for example, I am strong, I am kind, I am helpful, I am funny, I am determined, I am enthusiastic. Think about occasions when they showed these. Enable them to see the positive in themselves.

Feel blessed instead of stressed: Our children deal with a lot of stress, and stress is the enemy of positivity. The research says we cannot be stressed and thankful at the same time, so any time they are feeling stressed, encourage them to remember something they are thankful for and push the stress away.

Think of your child's mind as a garden. Help them to weed out the negative thoughts, and plant and nurture the positive thoughts. The garden will not become beautiful overnight, but slowly over a week, a month, a year, a lifetime, the garden will grow healthier and more vibrant. Take the time to nurture them with lots of love and positive energy and you will watch them flower.

Highlighting the positive without suggesting the negative

When he was seven, our son had to go to hospital to have an operation. The children's hospital was fantastic. We went on a visit first to see the ward and Chico the puppet showed us all the steps that the children would go through to get a general anaesthetic. The ward had a play area complete with video games and lots of books and toys. The staff went out of their way to make the environment and experience as stress-free as possible for the children. On the day, there was a play therapist on the ward to spend time with the children and be with them and their parents on the way to the operating theatre. She was a lovely lady, but I noticed very quickly that her interactions brought my son right down. He has extreme anxiety and was understandably scared about the operation. My husband and I were focused on keeping his anxiety down, keeping him occupied, and entertaining him and he was doing well, looking relatively relaxed and calm. However, each time the play therapist came over she would bring him back to feeling scared and his mood would plummet. She asked him questions such as, 'What are you most scared about?' and, 'You look much less scared now. On a scale of 1 to 10, how scared were you when you came in? And how scared are you now?' Her intention was entirely positive. She wanted to help him feel comfortable. She clearly loved her job and was focused on the children and making the experience a good one for them. The result of some of her interactions was the opposite of her intentions though. Her words put things in the negative, turned our son's focus to his fear and brought his mood down.

To me, this was a great illustration of why keeping the focus on the positive matters, and how important our language is and the power that words have over our mood. Our son's experience would have been different if the play therapist had reflected the positive to him, if she had talked about how good it would be after the operation, about the toast he would get later, about the cool toys that they had and what fun he could have with them. Luckily, we were able to bring him back up and support him to feel as positive as he could.

When our children are experiencing a big emotion, we still want to validate it. In this case, at the points when we could see that our son was feeling scared, we talked about it. We helped him manage what he was feeling and regulate himself. Highlighting the positive does not mean that we ignore the negative, but it does mean that we do not suggest it. We take our lead from what our children show us.

Chapter 6

DEALING WITH BIG EMOTIONS

The bodies, brains and nervous systems of children who have experienced trauma will have developed differently. Their brain chemistry will be different. They are likely to have difficulty identifying and managing emotions. They may internalize their feelings and suppress them, which can lead to anxiety or anger. Holding these feelings inside takes a lot of effort and sometimes the feelings can just bubble over, out of control. Being safe and feeling safe are not the same, so even though they are now in a safe environment, their brains and bodies may not recognize that the danger is no longer present. Their responses will have become habitual, and it will take time and lots of repetition for a child to learn that they can relax.

What lies beneath

To understand what is going on for our children, we need to understand a little about their brains and what is going on inside their heads. Put simply, there is a primitive, survival brain and wrapped around it is the thinking brain. The primitive brain runs on instinct and is focused on survival. It controls basic body functioning like breathing and digestion, our fight, flight, freeze or fawn responses and the big emotions like anger and fear. The higher brain manages thinking, decision making, planning and problem-solving, and regulates emotions and understanding of ourselves and the world.

The primitive brain is developed at birth; however, the higher brain develops throughout childhood and does not fully function until we are in our mid-twenties! Throughout childhood and into early adulthood, the higher brain is under construction. The reasoning part of the brain does not start to develop till age five at the earliest, so before that point, understanding big emotions is not possible for children. Even up to seven or eight, children are still in the preliminary stages of learning to manage their emotions, and for children who have experienced early life trauma this can take even longer. As parents, we want to enable our children to integrate the two parts of the brain: to develop the skills to make good decisions, control their emotions and develop empathy. For them to make good choices, we need both parts involved.

The primitive brain has a drive for survival. It acts like an alarm centre to keep us safe. If it senses danger, it shuts down the connection to the higher brain to allow us to act at speed. It aids our survival by acting purely on instinct, without thinking and analyzing getting in the way. This is extremely helpful in a real emergency, for example falling out of a tree, where instinctive responses will enable you to slow your fall by grabbing branches, or avoiding a collision on a bike by reacting in a split second. These responses are lifesaving; however, if the primitive brain is on high alert much of the time (as it is with our children) then it can cause challenges.

For example, if a child is bumped in a corridor at school, the primitive brain may interpret this as danger and shut down the higher brain. This cuts off all higher function. The child is operating purely at a primitive level. This leads to fight, flight or freeze responses, none of which are helpful in this situation. Adults may then attempt to reason with a child who has no access to reasoning and who after the event may have no clear memory of it. Within the child's brain, this was a purely instinctual response; a threat was detected, and the brain took action to preserve life. They did not make a choice, they reacted.

Sometimes feelings can build up and our children can feel overwhelmed, swamped by huge feelings that their brain is not yet mature enough to handle, and tipped into their primitive survival brain. At these points, even the simplest requests will be too much. They may show their connection to the person they are closest to by releasing these big emotions in their presence. It is an expression of trust, although it may seem like disconnection. When they most need that connection, they are likely to push it away. They may say they hate us, hit out or throw things. That is our cue to show them that we are there and connect with them; to help them feel safe and loved. If your child is overwhelmed, be with them in a calm way. Let them know that you are there for them, speak calmly and softly and reassure them that they are not having to face these big emotions alone. Give them the space they need but ensure that they know you are there for them too. Perhaps just sit near them, or by the door. Let them know you are there when they want you. Do not force interaction; let them initiate it.

If you can talk to them, support them to breathe into the feelings rather than pushing them away or ignoring them. Help them to see that the emotion will pass, to see that it is like a wave, and they can surf the wave. It will go up and that might feel scary, but it will come down too. Help them to see that this will pass.

Meeting the underlying need

As we have already seen, the brain continues to develop through to the early twenties, with the primitive brain developing first, followed by the higher brain. Adults often have expectations of children that they are not yet able to achieve. Then when the children do not meet these unrealistic expectations, it is labelled as bad behaviour. We are treating them as if they *won't* do it, when in fact they *can't* do it. Children are not mini-adults. Their brains are not fully developed, they do not see the big picture and struggle with cause and effect. It is our job to manage our expectations and to ask our children to do things that they *can* do at the level that they are at.

The behaviours that we see are only the tip of the iceberg, what we see on the surface. Like an iceberg, so much that underlies a child's behaviour is hidden from view. Behaviour is driven by feelings which are triggered by the deep-rooted needs of the child, their basic needs like feeling safe and secure, having sufficient sleep and food, being understood, being able to trust others, and feeling loved and as if they belong.

Behind every behaviour there is a feeling and behind every feeling there is a need.

When a child's basic needs are met, they will feel connected, safe and confident. However, a child whose early needs have not been met may feel insecure, afraid, angry or detached. This manifests on the surface as behaviours which the world may see as unacceptable as the child seeks to satisfy their unmet needs. The child's needs are valid, but their behaviours may not be helping them to meet these needs. In fact, they may be making things worse.

Outwardly, the world sees aggression, anger, controlling behaviour, bullying and shouting from the fight response. Or anxiety, panic, running away or storming off from the flight response. Or silence, refusal, numbness, indecision and withdrawal from the freeze response. Or people-pleasing and saying sorry over and over from the fawn response. All of these are symptoms of the deeper things below the surface. What we see is only a small part of what is there.

Under the surface are the underlying beliefs and emotions. They may be feeling vulnerable, hurt, disappointed, frustrated, jealous, anxious, scared – a mix of emotions. They may believe that they cannot cope, that the world is against them, that they are not good enough or are unloved. These are deep-seated beliefs about the world and themselves forged in their early years. These feelings and beliefs are hard to share, and the child may not even be aware of them consciously. We need to consider all the factors under the waterline, our child's underlying needs and feelings, rather than reacting to the behaviour that we see above the surface. Check in with them, connect and show that you love them and are there for them. Sometimes a hug is all that is needed.

Let them know that you can see it is hard for them, that you care about how they feel and that it is okay to feel these big feelings. Acknowledge and accept that they are feeling bad. Remind them that you love them no matter what and that you are there for them. Let them know that you will stay with them, that they are safe.

When they feel able, help them to explore the underlying needs by asking open, curious questions like these that validate their emotions:

- What is going on for you right now?
- How are you doing?
- How long have you been feeling like this?
- It sounds as though you are feeling…
- What I hear you saying is… Did I get that right?
- What can I do to help?
- I am sorry you are feeling this way, could we think about this together?
- Is there anything I am missing? Or anything else?

Listen without judgement or trying to fix things. Hear their point of view and validate that this is tough for them. Sometimes it might seem trivial to us, but it is big for them. Or it might trigger things in us that make us emotional. In the heat of the moment, ignore the behaviour and focus purely on the emotion. Do not try to rationalize with them, as their higher brain is unavailable. If talking about the emotion is too much for them at that moment, then empathize by saying, 'I can see you have had a tough day' or, 'I can see things are hard for you right now.' They may try to push you away, or tell you to go away, but remember that they are in survival mode and their brain may be seeing everything (including you) as a threat. Give them the space they need but stay close and keep checking in to convey the message that you hear that they are in pain and are there when they are ready and that you care. In time, the emotion will peak and they will be ready to connect.

Although in the moment we want to ignore the behaviour, sometimes if it is an issue of safety, or you need to address it for another reason, then come back to it later when everyone is calm and more able to talk in a constructive way. Remember that the behaviour is coming from a place of fear and self-protection, so focus on what could be done to change things next time rather than punishment or sanctions. These will not change things; the only way things will change is when the unmet need is addressed.

Whenever your child talks about difficult emotions, thank them for sharing and acknowledge that this would have been tough for them. Being vulnerable is hard, but worth it. Enable them over time to understand what is under the surface and once the underlying needs are met, the unwanted behaviour will go away by itself.

Seeing the emotion not the behaviour

Understanding that a behaviour is only what we see on the surface and that there is a lot more under the waterline that helps us to react in a way that enables our children to deal with it. When our children are struggling with big emotions, their behaviours can lead to them being seen as bad and adults turn to punishment as a response. When we can see the behaviours as a result of their distress, then we can react appropriately in a way that supports them to manage their inner pain. We address the emotion rather than the behaviour.

In the heat of the moment, that can be easier said than done as the behaviour is very visible and the emotion behind it is hidden. A useful technique is to think about what emotion your child is feeling and imagine that emotion in a bubble above their head. For example, 'I am anxious.'

Imagining the bubble helps us remember what is going on inside – it brings the emotion into view. This helps us to move past the behaviour and react to the emotion to meet the inner need.

Responding rather than reacting

Our children may have experienced chaotic lives and so may feel safer in a chaotic environment. They may seek to meet their needs by being loud, aggressive, controlling and demanding. It can be easy to get sucked into reacting in the same way and then things can escalate quickly. So how do we keep ourselves calm and not join in with the storm?

Thinking ahead and planning is a helpful way to prepare for situations which come up regularly, considering options in advance and thinking of a strategy about how you are going to respond and what you are going to say. It might be about being in a tag team with a partner, or, if you are on your own, taking a moment to yourself or calling on someone who can support you. It is about being responsive rather than reactive. When we are reactive, our cup gets full and overflows, as we are using our primitive brain. When we are responsive, we are using our thinking brain. We are taking a moment to think about what is going on.

Parenting our children is not just about the moment, it is also about prevention and reflection.

Ahead of time, we take the opportunity to plan and prepare. We think ahead, we establish boundaries and we create structure and routine. In the moment, we are present with them, we connect, we validate their feelings and are curious about what is going on for them. After the moment, we reflect. We think about what went well, what we can do more or less of and what we can change. We use that reflection to do things differently another time.

Reflecting and learning

What are the things to think about so we can learn from this situation and plan for the next?

Think about what they are trying to say. All behaviour is communication. When your child does something, take time to think about why they might be doing it. What are they trying to communicate to you? Do they need something from you to meet their needs? Are they feeling anxious, hungry or scared? Has something triggered them to a negative place? What happened just before the behaviour? Have you seen this before?

How can you meet the need? Sometimes children have emotional outbursts when their needs are not met. This could be something they need added, such as hugs, attention, food or sleep, or if things are too overwhelming it might mean taking things away: less noise, less busyness, less stimulation. Being responsive to your child is about tuning into them and giving them what they need to be happy and successful.

What could you have done differently ahead of time? Thinking ahead to the next time a similar situation could arise helps with putting things in place to get a better outcome next time. What were the triggers for them? Could they have been better prepared for the situation? Did they need more time for the transition? Would it have been better if they had eaten beforehand? Slept beforehand? Thinking about what we would change if we had this time again helps us to change things for the next time. The more we learn and the more of these little changes we make, the less often outbursts will happen. It is not about berating yourself for what you have done – quite the opposite – it is about learning and thinking about how you could react another time in a way that would be more helpful.

When we take the time to recognize and understand a child's point of view, we can understand the communication that lies behind the behaviour. Understanding the reason behind a behaviour makes it easier to react in a way that meets their needs and strengthens the connection.

How does this work in practice?

When my children were younger, we used to drive into school together every morning. Inevitably, we would be in a rush to leave the house, and everyone would be feeling stressed and anxious. Sometimes we would leave later than usual. Leaving later meant that the traffic was worse so we would end up arriving even later. These mornings my stress levels would increase very quickly, and the kids would end up running out of the car flustered and dysregulated. Their school day would start badly, and things would sometimes snowball throughout the day, creating bigger and bigger problems.

After one particularly stressful morning, I sat down when I got home and thought about school mornings and how they could be better.

First, I thought about the moments at home before we left. What were the trigger points? For us, a big one was getting out of the door with everything we needed. I made some visual reminders of what the kids needed for school each day and we started using these as part of the bedtime routine to get everything laid out and ready or packed in schoolbags. That took some of the pressure off before we left and made the exit from home much quicker and less frantic.

Then I thought about how I reacted to lateness. It is a big trigger for me, so I needed to be aware of this and think of ways to manage my reactions, as my anxiety was escalating things. I thought about ways I could calm myself in the moment and how I could adapt my behaviour to be a calming influence.

Quite soon after this, we got stuck in bad traffic and I knew we were going to be extremely late for school. I could feel my stress levels rising. However, because I had thought about it ahead of time, I chose to respond rather than react. I knew that what I had done previously was not working so I chose to do something else. I took a few deep breaths, told myself it was fine to be late, I could not change it so I needed to just accept it. When I felt more regulated, I started to play a spotting game with the kids in the car. Who can spot something red and stripey? Who can see the word 'sun'? We took turns and enjoyed ourselves. We were still stuck in traffic, we were still just as late, but we had fun. Not only did the stress levels reduce but we built a sense of unity, of being a family, of having good times together, and the kids went into school relaxed and happy. Win-win!

Dealing with toxic shame

Shame is a powerful emotion that can cause people to feel defective, unacceptable, even damaged beyond repair. From birth, babies are learning about the world and their place in it. Their sense of self is shaped by their life experiences. Children who are not taken care of in early life will internalize this and develop a belief that they were not cared for because they are undeserving, inadequate or inferior. They feel that it is their fault, and they are not worthy of love. Shame becomes part of their identity.

Shame is different from guilt. When we feel guilty, the guilt is about something specific that we have done. The thing is external to us, so we can take steps to make it right and move on. When we feel shame, we feel that we are wrong, that our whole self is wrong. This is much harder to put behind us.

The sense of shame that develops from experiences of complex trauma quickly becomes core to a young person's identity. Feelings of shame lead to feelings of anger and controlling behaviours. The child is unable to regulate their emotions and feels that they are never good enough. The shame has become toxic and underpins everything that they do. Consequently, the only way we can help traumatized young people to change their behaviours is to work with their sense of shame.

Feeling shame is uncomfortable. Children will build up defences to avoid feeling it. They may act tough and say they do not care. They may tell lies or blame others. They may become aggressive as their fear overtakes them. They may minimize what has happened, or their brains may have shut down in an act of self-protection. Traditional behavioural management strategies will only increase this shame and make things worse. Parents and other adults need to connect with the child and the emotions that they are experiencing to help the child to regulate their feelings of shame.

Think about connection, not correction. If they feel that their worries and fears are understood, then they will feel more able to lower their defences. When we reconnect with them, they learn that relationships can always be repaired, and that they are loved unconditionally.

Separate the behaviour from the child. Help them to see that they may have done something that was wrong but that does not make *them* wrong.

Avoid blaming them. Do not ask questions like, 'What did you do?' or, 'Did you smash the window?' Instead, ask open and curious questions such as, 'Tell me what happened' or, 'How did the ball get there?'

See it as a learning experience. Talk about choices, good and bad choices, and what could be better next time.

Let them show that they are sorry rather than saying it. They can do this by their behaviour or their demeanour. If we can see that they are sorry, that is positive and is enough.

If saying sorry is demanded at school, then think of creative ways to enable your children to comply without forcing them into a shame situation. We had a little pocket card that said, 'I did it, I am sorry' with a sad emoji face that could be shown to a teacher rather than having to say it aloud.

Speak calmly and come down to their level. Sitting parallel can help too.

We are made up of lots of parts

Children who feel shame and have low self-esteem may have an all-or-nothing mentality around identity. They may see themselves as all bad and others as all good. They may see themselves as the reason for their trauma. They can feel responsible for all the negative things that have happened in their lives. Helping children who think in a black and white way to see themselves as more complex enables them to move away from this destructive view of themselves and others. A powerful way to approach this is to talk to them about how we are all a combination of lots of different parts, some good, some not so good. Everyone is complicated, we are made up of many different skills, talents, emotions and beliefs and sometimes we are full of contradictions. We can be lots of things all at once.

Ideally do this in a physical way so there is something they can see and refer to later. You can draw a gingerbread man shape on a piece of paper, or if you have some large paper, you could draw around your child. Do one for yourself too, share the experience, share your positive and negative parts to help them see this is true of everyone. We did ones for all the members of the family and even did ones for the pets. The dog was mostly an eating part with a quite big sleeping part too!

Positive parts could be things like a kind part, a happy part, a helping part, a fun part, a smiley part, a smart part. They could be things the child is good at too, such as a footballing part, a finding things part, a drawing part, or a reading part. Make sure that there are lots of positive parts. It is about making them feel better about themselves and seeing things in perspective.

When looking at more negative parts, share yours first. Normalize having less positive parts – we all have them, so help them to see that it is okay. Negative parts could be things like an angry part, a hitting part, a bad words part, a shouty part, a mean part.

Make the size of the parts represent how much of them this part is. Talk about how the parts fit together. For example, 'Sometimes when your worried part wakes up it gets your angry part involved' or, 'Your kind part and your helpful part come along together.'

Once you have established using this sort of language it gives you the opportunity to talk about things in a constructive way. For example, 'I can see you are using your concentrating part there, and your smart part too, great effort' or, 'I can't find my car keys, can you bring your eagle eye spotting part to help me find them?' or, 'I think you need to ask your calm part to help because I can see your worried part is starting to wake up your angry part.' Using parts language gives us the opportunity to add light and shade to how we describe things, and to their view of themselves. Enabling our children to understand that they are made up of many parts helps them to see that they are more than one thing. This helps them to move away from the crippling toxic shame that they may feel and see the world and themselves in a more nuanced light.

Teaching our children to help themselves

Children can sometimes feel helpless and as if things are out of their control. They may feel that big emotions take them over and there is nothing that they can do. Talking through strategies that match individual emotions is a wonderful way to engage your child in realizing that they have a choice. If they feel a certain way, there are things they can do to change it. Knowing that they can take some control is empowering. Work through the options with them, making them personal to them. It can help to talk about concrete situations with them if they are finding talking in the abstract too difficult. Here are a few examples of feelings and possible strategies to give you some ideas to start the ball rolling:

When I feel sad I can...

- find someone to give me a cuddle
- do something active to get my blood pumping
- look at pictures of me having a fun time
- speak to a family member or friend
- do something kind for someone else.

When I feel shy I can...

- team up with someone to help me talk
- think of something I can say about the other person
- smile and look welcoming, or say hello
- remember that everyone feels shy sometimes.

When I feel grumpy I can...

- do something I enjoy
- go outside and let the air take my grumpiness away
- look at pictures of me having a fun time
- imagine I am in a lovely place and go there in my head.

When I feel angry I can...

- take deep breaths
- think about floating away on a cloud of calmness
- go for a walk
- do something active to burn off the angry feelings
- think of something I am grateful for.

When I feel scared I can...

- take deep breaths until I feel calmer
- imagine the thing I am scared of with a funny voice, running away and getting smaller and smaller
- say to myself, 'I am scared but I can do this'
- find someone to be with and do it together.

Surfing the wave of emotion

When we feel a strong negative emotion, the temptation is either to push it away or react on impulse. Neither response is helpful. There is another more resourceful way to deal with big emotions like sadness and anger. Think about the feeling as being like waves in the sea. Think about being on a surfboard on top of the wave, riding the wave in the knowledge that it will only last a little while and then it will subside. Some waves are higher and stronger than others, but they always break on the shore. The feeling is temporary. It will pass. Helping our children to recognize their emotions, to accept them and know that they will go away is a powerful tool to manage strong emotions in a resourceful way.

So how do teach our children to surf the wave?

First, we need to support them to recognize what they are feeling – to name it and accept that it is okay to feel this; to think about the feeling as being within them, part of them, but not all of them. They can experience the emotion, ride it out. Like a wave, they cannot stop it or hold on to it and there is no point in trying. It is about going with the flow, observing the feeling, thinking about it, being curious. Where is it in their body? Is it a particular colour? A shape? Is it moving or still? Is it heavy or light? Is there a sound? Or a smell? They can be conscious of it, not pushing it away or holding on to it, just letting it wash over them. If it feels too much, get them to remember times when they felt positive emotions, knowing that this is not how they will always feel, this is temporary. Like a wave, the feeling will break and wash away. This too will pass.

STOP	BREATHE INTO THE FEELING Where is it? What is it like?	ACCEPT IT It is okay to feel this way. This is just how it is. It will pass.	KEEP BREATHING INTO THE FEELING Is it moving? Is it changing?	NOTICE IT FADING

SURFING THE WAVE OF EMOTION

When they learn to accept how they feel, to experience the emotion and know that it will pass, they can surf the wave of the emotion and come out the other side with better skills to surf the next one.

Regulation and dysregulation

Children are not born with the ability to regulate themselves. These coping skills develop as the child models the regulation skills of the adults around them. A child whose initial years may have been with a caregiver who was dysregulated will not have had the opportunity to develop healthy regulation skills and will themselves be dysregulated. When a child is dysregulated, they may react in ways that seem to the observer to be out of proportion to the situation. They may struggle with impulse control and may become overwhelmed and unable to calm down. In these moments, they are unable to access their higher brain and manage their behaviours or choices. They are operating at a primitive brain level and are either over-aroused in a fight or flight response, or under-aroused in a freeze or flop response. They can get stuck in their primitive survival brain, seeing threats everywhere, constantly in alert mode, hypervigilant to everything around them. When a child is stuck in their primitive brain, they are not accessing the higher areas of the brain which are crucial for learning and development.

Self-regulation is the ability to manage your emotions and your behaviours in line with the situation you are in. It is the ability to calm yourself, to manage emotions like disappointment, anger, frustration and sadness. Self-regulation is important in every facet of our children's lives. It enables our children to succeed in school, at home and with friends. It helps them cope with big emotions, learn from experience and feel good about themselves and what they can achieve.

Always seek to build regulation before expecting anything of your child. A dysregulated child will have difficulty listening. It is not a behaviour problem; it is not that they will not listen. It is a regulation issue because they cannot process what you are saying.

Children who find regulation difficult will often be in too high a state of arousal where they become anxious, angry or overwhelmed, or in too low an arousal state where they are shutting down.

When we are over-aroused, we are in a fight or flight state, with high energy and activity which often manifests as hypervigilance, anxiety, fear, anger or meltdown. All systems are stuck in the 'on' position, making it hard to relax, sleep, eat or regulate emotions. Sometimes, over-arousal can be so overwhelming to the brain that it causes disconnection and shutdown, tipping over into under-arousal.

When we are under-aroused, we are in a freeze response with associated feelings of numbness, shutdown or disassociation. All systems are stuck in the 'off' position, making us want to sleep all the time, not eat and we may feel emotionally switched off.

In the over- or under-arousal states, we are less able to process what is going on around us as the higher thinking brain shuts down and the capacity of rational thought and decision making is unavailable. When we are within the calm arousal zone, we are 'just right' and feel able to cope with the ups and downs of daily life.

Understanding the signs when our child is moving towards the top of the calm zone and nearing over-arousal, and helping them to understand and notice these signs, is a valuable tool in developing self-regulation. Knowing that they are close to tipping into over-arousal gives the opportunity to make changes before they become completely dysregulated. Each child will have different triggers and visible signs, but look out for energy and noise levels rising. Look for wiggly, increasing body activity levels, silliness, fewer kind words. They might feel other things internally too; things like an increased heart rate, rising temperature or a feeling of things speeding up. The more you both understand the signs, the more able you (and they) will be to self-regulate.

RED ZONE: OVER-AROUSED (MANIC)

Fight/flight/fawn response

Anxious, angry, hypervigilant, feeling unsafe, racing thoughts, overwhelmed, feeling out of control

> Looks like: Angry face, kicking, punching, hitting, fighting, over eager, hyper aware, super compliant
>
> Sounds like: Yelling, crying, talking fast and loudly, banging things
>
> Feels like: Angry, overwhelmed, out of control, not able to think, desperate to please

GREEN ZONE: CALM AROUSAL (JUST RIGHT)

The zone where you can cope with challenges – the optimal place to be connected, flexible, relaxed and ready to learn

> Looks like: Smiling, able to listen and learn, focused
>
> Sounds like: Using kind words, calm voices
>
> Feels like: Calm, happy, peaceful

BLUE ZONE: UNDER-AROUSED (SHUTDOWN)

Freeze response

Zoned out, numb, ashamed, passive, frozen and disconnected from the world

> Looks like: Head down, still, yawning, shutdown
>
> Sounds like: Sad, bored, silent
>
> Feels like: No energy, everything in slow motion, feeling empty

If a child's arousal levels are reducing, they may appear tired, lethargic or distracted. They may have a more slumped posture than usual or be quieter or stiller than normal. Raising levels of arousal is about increasing the sensory input. This can be done with any physical activity like running or jumping, or singing or dancing along with a favourite song to raise the mood. Crunchy foods give a strong sensory input too. Food like carrots, apple and popcorn are good. Cold foods like frozen fruit, ice cubes or cold water help too, as they enliven the senses.

Outbursts can sometimes appear to come out of nowhere, and other times the build-up is visible until finally the meltdown happens.

Sometimes it can be something seemingly small that triggers it. Sometimes the trigger appears to be something that our child has dealt with many times before. We search for underlying causes and frequently are unable to see the pattern. There will sometimes be an identifiable trigger that tips our child into over- or under-arousal, but often it will be several things that have built up over time that have caused it.

I like to use the metaphor of filling up a bucket when I think about our children's (and our) calm zone and the ability to regulate. There is a finite amount of space in the bucket, and it can suddenly overflow. Each negative thing that happens in a day might add a little to the bucket, each positive thing might empty a little out. Some things will add or remove lots of water, others just a drop. Some of the things will be in the world around us, others will come from our internal world.

For children who have experienced early life trauma, their bucket may be almost full before they start their day. It may already be brimming with shame, self-loathing and sensory overwhelm. They may only have a sliver of space available before they tip over into overwhelm.

When the bucket is already quite full, it only takes a small drip to cause the overflow. The ability to cope is dependent on how much space there is left in the bucket. It is helpful to think about it in this way because when we look for a trigger that led to an outburst it may seem that there is not anything big that we can see. This can seem confusing as our children may cope with things with seeming ease at one point, when at other times something much smaller overwhelms them.

What adds to each person's bucket and what takes water out is very personal; however, here are some ideas to get you started thinking about your child's bucket, and your own too.

What fills up the bucket?

There are big things:

- change
- transitions
- sensory overstimulation
- negative emotions like shame and guilt
- anything that creates anxiety
- feeling out of control
- trauma triggers.

And small ones:

- getting something wrong
- feeling embarrassed or left out
- feeling tired or frustrated
- niggling sensory things like clothes labels rubbing or a scent that is not agreeable.

It all adds up...

What reduces how full the bucket is?

- doing enjoyable things
- calming breaths
- being rested
- being fed and watered
- feeling supported and having a connection to another person
- doing something physical to get the body's stress levels down
- focusing on something positive or creative
- sensory stimulation such as weighted blankets or heavy pressure
- being with animals or in nature
- rhythmic activity to soothe the nervous system
- singing or dancing.

It all takes away...

Using the bucket metaphor helps them (and us) see that there are strategies that will help and this in turn helps both of us feel more in control. It is about finding a balance, helping them to find ways to avoid things that add to the bucket where possible while at the same time identifying things that empty their bucket. The lower the base level, the less often overflow will happen. Knowing about their bucket and how it works can also help them to recognize when their bucket is getting full and to have strategies to empty some out.

The more we support our children to self-regulate, the less they will tip into over- or under-arousal and the more they will be able to function effectively and reflect and learn.

Scaffolding to support success

As we have seen, our children's ability to cope is related to how full their bucket is. Positive experiences empty a little out of their bucket, whereas stressors will fill it up. They need to feel good about themselves, feel proud so that their bucket stays at a manageable level, and then they will have the space to raise the level a little when things get tough without it overflowing. When they are anxious and their bucket is filling up, we need to give them space, keep demands low and give them time to come to us. We want to ensure that the level of demand (schoolwork, activities, expectations) we place on our children is in relation to the space they have available in their bucket. When we support them to succeed, they learn that they are capable, they feel proud, and this builds resilience and helps them to regulate themselves.

Feelings first, then logic: Remember that when they are dysregulated, your child's primitive brain is in charge. They are overwhelmed and have no control or access to reflection or understanding. Realize that in these moments they need connection, acceptance and empathy. There will be time later to learn and practise regulation skills.

Build exposure to situations: When we know that a particular situation is hard for our children, it is tempting to avoid it. However, that does not teach our children how to handle these situations and may feed into your child's inner narrative that they cannot cope. Instead, help them to face the situation but ensure that it is in a controlled way with a supportive framework around it so that they succeed and, in the process, learn skills that they can use the next time.

For example, our son was terrified of fireworks. He would cower and freeze if he heard them outside the house, even when he was safely indoors. We started showing him firework displays on a tablet. We learned about lots of different types of fireworks and how they were made. When there were fireworks nearby, we watched from the window. Eventually we went to a local firework display at a location that he knew well and where he felt safe, and ensured that we were sitting in a rugby stand with a roof so he would feel more enclosed. We also took ear defenders so he could cope better with the noise. It took a while, but eventually he felt comfortable with fireworks. At each stage, he learned that he could do it and that gave him confidence to face the next step. He also learned that even when we fear something, if we do it a little at a time then we can overcome the fear.

Let them do it with a safety net: We want to help and support our children. However, when we hover over them ready to help, we are taking over the regulation role. We are not giving them the space they need to find their own coping strategies. A child may not be able to do the whole of a task themselves, but if we break it down so that they can do some of it, then as time goes on, they will be able to manage more and more steps. For example, if they are doing maths homework, you could help them get settled and do part of a question with them, then leave them to do the rest themselves. If you are nearby but 'busy', then you can listen in just in case they become audibly frustrated and you can suggest ways they could manage their frustration. Say something like, 'When I feel frustrated, I get up and pour myself a glass of water. I find moving a little and getting hydrated helps me come back to the problem more able to solve it.' This helps them to regulate themselves and learn a strategy to use the next time. They are practising self-regulation but doing it with the support of a safety net.

Have a practice run: When your child is anxious about something, or where it has led to meltdowns in the past, do a practice run at a time where the stakes are lower and the whole focus is on them succeeding. For example, our son was starting a club at the local army barracks after school. All the children were going to walk up together with a teacher and although he was desperate to go, he was really scared because of the armed sentry guard on the gate and the unfamiliar surroundings. To show him that he could do it, we broke it down into lots of little steps. We talked it through first and highlighted all the bits of the walk he had already done at other times. Then we drove it slowly. Then we walked it with the dogs to take the pressure off. Finally, we arranged to meet the helper the week before at the barracks so he could go in with her and get familiar with the setting. She had primed the sentries who were expecting us, and they chatted to him and let him see that they were just people and that they were friendly. It took several steps, each with a limited exposure so he could manage his regulation and, in the end, he was confident in his ability to do it by himself.

Break it down: Some activities can be broken down into lots of smaller steps. Breaking them down enables our children to experience success at each step and build confidence. For example, if your child likes to bake, then, using a simple recipe, work through it in stages, developing their skills and coping strategies. The first time, get all the ingredients out and weigh things together, but let them do the mixing. Next time, you can get out the ingredients and they can do the weighing and the mixing. The following time, they can get the ingredients too. Where you are helping, if they are getting frustrated or struggling with regulation, help them to think of strategies to manage their emotions. Eventually they will be doing it all themselves (although depending on their age, you may want to put it in the oven for them).

Do it virtually: There are lots of resources available online to visit places virtually ahead of a trip in real life. We were going on the sleeper from Edinburgh to London recently and ahead of the trip looked at photos and videos of the train and carriages to make it familiar. By the time we got on, it felt as if we had done it lots of times already.

Try it first with a less emotionally challenging option: Where a child is struggling to manage something, help them to practise doing it at a lesser intensity. Once they have mastered that then they can try it at progressively greater levels. For example, if your child struggles with the transition away from playing a computer game, try doing the transition first with a game that they like less, or have practice runs of stopping and starting by coming off the game for a short period of time. Perhaps start with a minute and over time work up in increments. In this way, they build tolerance alongside coping and regulation skills to enable them to handle the bigger transition.

Managing trauma triggers

A trigger is a reminder of a past trauma. This reminder can cause sudden overwhelming emotions and may cause a flashback so that the child relives the negative memory. The response to a trauma trigger will often materialize purely as a reaction with no associated memory. The child has no understanding of why this sudden big emotional response has happened, which can make it seem more frightening.

If your child responds in a way that is extreme and unexpected, consider that they may be experiencing a trauma trigger. Often their responses to a situation may be seen as bad behaviour when it is a learned response to bad things that have happened to them. A trigger can be external, such as a smell, a sound, a taste, a person or a location. Or it can be internal, such as a particular emotion or a feeling in the body. It can be anything that creates a link for the child to a traumatic event from their past. It takes the child directly back to the moment in their mind. Their brain and body is overwhelmed by reliving the traumatic memory. How your child reacts will depend on whether they go into a fight, flight, freeze or fawn response. They could either melt down or shut down.

If your child has a sudden trauma response, ensure that they are safe and that they know that they are safe. Sit with them and reassure them. Once they are calmer, if they feel able, it can help to talk through what they believe triggered the response, how they felt and where it took them to. Talk about how they are safe now and ensure that they understand that they are not responsible for what happened, that it was out of their control. If they do not feel able to talk, or understanding this is beyond them, do not push it. Let them deal with things in their own time. If you are concerned, seek out professional support to enable them to process these big feelings.

Learning to relax

Teaching our kids techniques to relax will support them throughout their lives. When they relax, it increases their endorphins to create a feel-good sensation, reduces cortisol levels to reduce their stress response and helps their bodies to support their immune system. When children learn techniques to relax, they can learn to self-regulate and manage their responses better – an amazing gift to give them to take through childhood and into adulthood.

Breathing for relaxation and regulation

It is important for health that we breathe as deeply as possible. Teaching our children to breathe deep down into the diaphragm encourages their lungs to take in more air, helping them to feel calmer and more relaxed, and develops concentration and clarity. Here are a few games that encourage deeper breathing:

Jellyfish breaths: For some children, the concept of taking a deep breath is difficult to understand. Create a visual aid of a jellyfish by cutting a paper plate in half, drawing a face on it, and adding long tissue streamers hanging from the cut side. Kids love to blow on the tentacles to make the jellyfish swim and it focuses their attention on their breath. Get them to inhale to a count of three and see how long they can exhale while still making the tentacles move.

Underwater breathing: Tell your child to imagine that that they are holding their breath underwater. Get them to breathe in, hold their nose, puff their cheeks out, then hold for a count of three. Get them to blow out slowly and smoothly and repeat two or three times.

Birthday candles: Get them to imagine that they are blowing out the candles on their birthday cake. They take a deep breath in, then breathe out little sharp breaths, one for each candle. Repeat two or three times.

Out with the old: Get them to take in a deep breath, put their lips together to make a small o, and let out a soft, slow, steady breath. See if they can blow out all the old air in their lungs. Now get them to take a deep breath, filling their lungs with new clean air. Repeat two or three times. For a nice alternative, get them to imagine breathing in and out sunshine or a favourite colour.

Happy bubble thoughts: Imagine that you are blowing happy thought bubbles of peace, happiness or love to each other. Slowly and gently blow the bubbles and imagine the room filling up with the happy thoughts.

Rocket breath: Take off into relaxation today! Explain to your child that you are going to practise a deep breath like a rocket. Start the inhale with their hands at their side, inhaling up to hands together above their head while you count down 10 to 1. Then for lift off, a big exhale with a whoosh as their arms come down.

Feathers: Get them to imagine blowing feathers into the room. They take a deep breath and as they breathe out, they blow the feathers softly into the air. Get them to imagine making them dance, to see how high and far they can blow them. Maybe try it with a real feather.

Fire breaths: Get them to imagine being a fire eater at the circus. As they breathe, get them to imagine breathing out flames of fire. How far will they go? How wide will the flames be?

Quick stress busters

When your child needs tension relief, try one of these techniques to do a quick state shift:

Put your feelings in a box: This is a great tool for your child to use when their feelings are overwhelming them. They grab their feelings (from their stomach or chest or wherever they feel they are) and put them into the box. The box can be real or imaginary. When they feel that all their scary feelings are in the box, they can put the lid on it and put them away either forever, or until they are feeling strong enough to face them.

Throw your feelings away: This is like putting feelings in a box, but instead your child draws or writes the feeling on paper then scrunches it up and throws it away.

Give or get a bear hug: When we hug, our bodies produce oxytocin, which is also known as the love hormone as it generates a feeling of connection. Even a short hug reduces blood pressure, increases feelings of well-being and reduces stress in both parties.

Count slowly: This can be combined with breathing techniques to make it even more effective.

Repeat a mantra: Together decide on a phrase that your child can repeat to themselves when they feel stressed to help them calm down. Something like, 'I am calm' or, 'I am relaxed' or, 'I can do it'. Make sure it resonates with your child and is positive (you do not want to get them thinking about what they do not want).

Whisper the alphabet: Reciting something familiar such as the alphabet is a good anxiety-reducing technique and whispering it helps them to focus on something other than their negative emotions in the moment.

Get active: Get them to do star jumps, bounce on a trampoline, run. Anything that burns energy will release endorphins and alter their mood.

Dance it away: Put on some music and have a dance. The more energetic the better to dance away the stresses and welcome in the calm.

Sing it away: Sing a favourite song loudly. Singing forces deeper breathing and remembering the lyrics focuses the mind away from the stressors. The act of singing aloud releases feel-good chemicals in the brain.

Yell it out: Do a primitive scream. You can even have a competition for who can do the most blood-curdling scream. Really put lots of noise behind it and yell all that negative energy out.

Head down, mood up: Bringing the head below the level of the heart is calming for the nervous system. So, encourage your child to do a handstand, touch their toes or do a head down yoga pose.

Drink water: When we are dehydrated, we are unable to operate well. Pour them a glass of water and have them sip it slowly.

When I feel upset, worried, or disappointed I can...
Create a visual of the regulation tools that your child could use. Include them in the creation. Add online pictures if your computer skills are up to it, or cut things out of magazines. Make it inviting, so they want to use the tools. Add things like do a silly dance, doodle, stretch, jump on a trampoline, go outside, write down how I feel, read a book, sing a song, take a big breath, go to my calm space, use my soothing box, do a puzzle. There are lots of other options within this section. Select ones they enjoy and will choose to do.

Making a visual representation gives them something to refer to and will help them remember that they have options when they start to feel wobbly. You can make different ones for home and school as their options may be different.

Tense and relax
Progressive muscle relaxation is a technique that circles around the body, tensing and relaxing muscles in turn. Play a game a few times, with your

child making their body stiff and straight like a soldier; get them to make every muscle held tight, then get them to go all soft and floppy like a rag doll or cooked spaghetti. Once they have the hang of tensing and relaxing over their whole body, you can progress to doing different muscles in succession.

Get them to lie flat on the floor or on a bed. Move round their body from shoulders to arms to tummy, legs and then toes. At each muscle group, get them to make it stiff and hold for five to ten seconds then to let it go all soft and floppy and breathe slowly in and out as they relax. After they have tensed and relaxed their toes, get them to wiggle different body parts to relax even more – their toes, their legs, their nose, eyebrows, anything they like.

Once your child has learned to tense and relax the whole body, the next step is to practise relaxing without tensing so that your child can easily use this strategy in a wide range of situations. Ask your child to take a deep breath, then slowly let out the breath while silently saying the word 'relax' and letting the whole body go limp like a rag doll. If the child wishes, they can go through several breaths, each time letting the body become looser and more relaxed after each breath. The goal is to help your child develop a quick strategy so that they can relax in any situation.

A self-soothe box

A self-soothe box is a fantastic way to enable your child to manage feelings of anxiety or overwhelm and help them feel more regulated and relaxed. Fill a box with items that they can pull out whenever they need them, which will give them the strategies and confidence to be able to manage their stress and anxiety on their own. Think about all the senses as you build it. You could include something to smell, something to touch, something to look at and even something to taste.

Sensory input: Include lots of things for them to touch to focus their hands and minds. Playdough, fidget cubes or spinners create a focus. Think about texture too, by adding distinct types of fabric and surfaces. Things that cause resistance are great, as the pressure helps the mind to relax and the muscles also learn how to relax as the pressure comes off. Stress balls, massage balls, chewing gum, resistance bands or stretchy fabric are good for this.

Positive memories: Include pictures of your child and friends and family having fun. Encourage them to see that they are loved and that how they feel in this moment is not how they feel at other times. Help them to see that this negative emotion will pass.

Comfort: Include a small favourite toy, or a thin blanket and pillow. Perhaps add a bottle of water, as sipping helps to regulate breathing.

Smell: Scented putty, or a lavender pillow or a roller bottle of a scent that they like is a fantastic way to change the mood. Hand cream is nice too, and the action of applying it is calming.

Sound: A little music box or player can be helpful to give your child another focus. Headphones can be helpful too, to enable them to be more immersed in the sound and distanced from distractions and irritations around them.

Activity: Having an activity to complete can really help with self-soothing. Colouring or small crafts are both rewarding and give the mind something constructive and creative to focus on. Doing something rhythmic such as drumming can also help.

Before introducing your child to their kit and its contents, sit down with them and discuss the signs that they are beginning to feel anxious. Have them describe to you the changes they feel in their body. Ask them questions about their heart rate, their breathing, their senses, their temperature (many children describe feeling hot or cold), and any other changes they notice in their bodies as they begin to become anxious. Introduce the kit that you have made 'just for them' and explain how each thing may be used when they start to feel anxious. Ask if there is anything else they think you should include. Some children like to decorate the box themselves to personalize it. Explain that they should use it in a quiet place. Encourage them to use it without having to ask you first but tell them that you will be there to help them when they use it initially, until they feel able to deal with using the box on their own. Talk to them about what it is like when you feel stressed and what sort of strategies you use to help yourself. Empower them to see that they are not the only ones dealing with stress.

A quiet space in the mind

When we think about things that are upsetting, our body tenses up. This is because the lower centres of our brain, which regulate body functions, do not distinguish between real images and those which are imagined. If you think about being in an uncomfortable situation, your body will begin to respond as if you were in that situation. Instead of your child imagining something that makes them feel uncomfortable, help them to imagine something that makes them feel good. Help them create a quiet space in their mind. Talk through with them what space they would imagine is their special happy place. A turret at the top of a castle, on a cloud floating by, on a beach, on the moon, or floating on a satellite.

Get them to relax and take a few deep breaths and imagine they are there. Get them to fully imagine being there. Get them to look around, to listen for sounds and identify smells. Get them to tune into everything about the experience: how it looks, sounds and feels. Get them to walk or look around their vision, describing it with all their senses. Help them to make it feel real to them.

When they are ready, ask them to lock the place up safely deep inside their mind, and let them know that they have the key and can go there whenever they choose. It is a wonderful thing for parents to do too. Take a brief mental holiday, a little piece of calm in an often-frantic world.

A quiet space in the real world

When a child is feeling overwhelmed, going somewhere safe and quiet is a fantastic way for them to regroup and regulate themselves. Having the option to choose to go to this quiet space gives your child the opportunity to take steps to regulate themselves and develop an understanding of their own need to stop and relax for a while. The space needs to be calming, and not too stimulating, closed off from the noise and bustle of the rest of the house. Ensure that the lighting is low (fairy lights work well), and that calming music is available, but if your child is easily overstimulated complete quiet may be better.

It does not need to be a big space, or a dedicated space. For example, you could put curtains around a lower bunk or make a den under the stairs. Include some sensory toys for fiddling with and a blanket or pillow so it is cosy. They could have their self-soothe box there. Make sure that there are some positive images in the box showing them being loved and part of the family. When you introduce your child to their quiet space, explain what is for and that it is just for them to use whenever they feel the need. To begin with you may want to encourage them to use the room when you feel they could benefit from it; in time you should find they begin to use it when they feel the need. You might also want to sit with your child sometimes, relax with them. This models behaviour, helps you connect, and you might find you really benefit from taking some time out too.

Mindfulness activities

Mindfulness is about paying full attention to something, slowing down to really notice what is happening. It helps with emotional regulation and cognitive focus. So how can we teach mindfulness to our children? Here are a few mindfulness techniques that work well with any age:

Funhouse mirrors: Stand facing each other, then move your body, and ask your child to mirror the movements. Watching and copying helps children listen, focus and stay present in the moment.

Breathing buddy: Have your child lie down on a mat on the floor, or on their bed, and place their favourite stuffed toy on their tummy. Have them rock the stuffed animal to sleep with the movement of their tummy as they breathe in and out. This helps them to pay attention to their breathing.

Go on a 'noticing' walk: Stroll along and notice things you have not seen before. For one minute of the walk, all be completely silent and you should pay attention to all the sounds you can hear – frogs, birds, an aeroplane, a lawnmower.

The Spider Man meditation: Get your child to activate their 'spidey-senses' and their ability to focus on all they can smell, taste and hear in the present moment.

Make a calm down jar: Fill a clear jar with water, food colouring, glitter and some clear or glitter glue. Shake it up and watch the glitter settle. The calm down jar is a bit like a snow globe – shake it up and watch the storm subside. The analogy is that if we sit and breathe and simply watch the disturbance, it settles, and our minds are like that too.

Practise mindful eating: The exercise of mindfully eating a raisin or a piece of chocolate is a staple of mindfulness education and is a great activity for kids. Do it together. Look at it closely, smell it, put it in your mouth and let it melt without sucking. What do you notice? What tastes, smells, textures, sensations? Take lots of time and focus fully on it. How do you feel about it compared with if you had eaten it mindlessly?

Co-regulation

Children who struggle with emotional regulation need help from a connected and accepting adult to enable them to transition to a calmer state. As parents, we are modelling our behaviours to our children all the time. We can support our children to regulate themselves by regulating ourselves, showing them that we feel anxious and narrating how we manage ourselves. We validate their feelings and share ours. We are present with them when they are dysregulated and we share some of our calm energy. Kids are like mirrors, reflecting our feelings and behaviours.

Young children are particularly sensitive to everything that we say or do. This makes it challenging for us as parents, because when we are struggling the most, our children will tune in and replay back our negative emotions, which can turn into a cycle of escalation. We can sometimes be pulled into their overwhelm and amplify it, even though that is not our intention. We can end up shouting at them to stop shouting, for example.

No matter how much we may wish to, we cannot take away their pain, but we can face it together, sitting with them and teaching them how to feel it. The more we show how we manage our own difficult feelings, the more our children will learn to regulate theirs.

Chapter 7

MANAGING BEHAVIOUR

Children who have experienced an environment of chaos and unpredictability need parents and homes that are consistent and predictable, where there are rules and expectations that are clear and understood. They need clear and consistent boundaries to keep them safe and to give them a sense of security. Without these limits, children feel insecure and can feel as if they can push their parents to do whatever they wish. Although this may seem as if they are getting what they want, in fact a child having this level of control can lead to them feeling anxious and insecure.

Children need limits, but they like to test them too, to push against boundaries and see where the edges are. This is how they learn new things, how they become more independent. It may be an important part of growing up, but for us parents, maintaining healthy boundaries against this push in a consistent way can be tiring and challenging. Being consistent matters though. When we set limits and stick to them, our children know what to expect and there will be less pushback.

Children thrive when they know what to expect. Having a clear set of rules within the family creates a framework of how the family behaves and can help everyone get along better. It is not about having an extensive list of dos and don'ts. It is about having a small number of clear, positive statements that state the behaviour we want to see, not the behaviour that we do not want. Every family's rules will be different; we each have different values and priorities and our rules will reflect the ages and stages of our children.

Rules could be things like:

- We say please and thank you.
- We put our coats and bags in the hall when we come in.
- We knock before coming into a bedroom.

Involve the whole family in agreeing the rules. Think about things like manners, behaviour towards each other, staying safe and chores around the house. The more children feel involved, the more they will buy-in. It can be helpful for the adults to have a think first, so you are not starting with a blank sheet of paper but making sure the process is collaborative. If you end up with too many then combine them if you can and only choose the most important ones to include. Once you have your list, put them up somewhere that everyone can see so you can refer to them frequently. Revisit them periodically to add new ones or remove or change ones that are not working or that are no longer appropriate for your children's ages.

Having family rules helps our children to know what to expect and helps us to be more consistent.

When we are consistent with our routines, rules, consequences and connection to our children, we set limits and boundaries for our children in a loving, therapeutic way so they know what to expect and learn to trust those around them, and the world seems more stable, predictable and secure. Having this structure around them helps them to take in and organize information and learn about the world around them.

When we have a set routine and stick to it, we set expectations and create a framework that we all understand. When things crop up that derail things, be open about this with your child. Explain why the changes are necessary and what the changes will be so that your child is prepared and will feel less anxious. Deal with any changes in a calm and measured way so your child can see that you are still in control, and get back on track as soon as you can.

Consistency is not just about one parent – both parents need to respond in similar ways so that our child knows what to expect and does not exploit cracks to set us up against each other. When parents are consistent, children know what is expected and can predict how we will react. They will still try to stretch the boundaries, to push our buttons, but in time they will be less likely to do so.

At the start, it can seem as if implementing consistent rules and boundaries is creating escalation. Children can push back to see if you will let things slide. Try to stay calm and hold your ground. When we give in because we are tired or do not want to rock the boat, it makes us unpredictable and unsettles our children, leading to anxiety and escalation.

Being consistent does not mean we can never be flexible. It means that we have a framework that we work within but when the need arises, we can forego it. However, when you do change things, choose those times carefully and explain the reason for the change. That way it is still predictable.

Our children need to know that we are there for them and that there are boundaries to feel safe. They need to understand that there are consistent rules and that we as parents are consistent. It is about us being the authority figure but not the boss. When we show that we are in charge and are calm and measured, we show our children that everything is okay and model how to behave in a calm way.

Children model their behaviour on how they see us behave. If we speak to them in a polite and respectful manner, then we show them that is how we would like them to behave. It is unrealistic to expect our children to behave in ways that we do not. The old maxim of 'do as I say, not as I do' does not work. Speak to your child in a measured, kind and friendly tone. Be firm and set clear boundaries in language they will understand.

Make your communication appropriate for your child's understanding and attention span. Having a prolonged discussion about the rights and wrongs of a particular action with a young child is pointless and can in fact be counterproductive as they will switch off and become disconnected. Keep it short and to the point. Do give reasons so your child knows why they are being asked to do something but make them simple. For example, 'You need to hold my hand in the car park because there are lots of cars around and I need to keep you safe.'

Do not expect your children to get it right the first time you ask them to do something, or get it right consistently either. Like us, they have good and bad days and will need lots of patience and support to learn a new skill or change a behaviour.

Parenting can be exhausting and frustrating. When we are feeling overwhelmed and just trying to make it to bedtime, it can be tempting to let consistency slide. Remember that we are all human, being consistent takes effort and repetition and we will not get it right all the time. When you slip up, take ownership of it, explain to your child that you got it wrong and start again with a clean sheet. Good enough is good enough.

Managing difficult behaviour

If our child is dysregulated, then the most important thing is to support them to manage these big emotions and come back to a calmer state. We always manage the connection with our child first.

Where our child reacts because they are overwhelmed and in a fight, flight or freeze state then their actions are out of their control. They are not acting on reason, but on instinct. In these instances, our immediate priority is safety – of themselves and of others. Then we can focus on helping them to feel calmer. Use some of the relaxation techniques in the previous chapter, such as breathing exercises, self-soothing or mindfulness activities to achieve this. Or sometimes a hug and just being there is what is needed.

Later we may want to work out what could have helped before they became overwhelmed so we can make things better another time, but our initial focus is on connection and regulation. Consequences are not appropriate in these situations; they are not responsible for their actions because they are in survival mode with no access to higher thought or reasoning. Consequences are only appropriate where a child had a choice.

There are plenty of times where our children will present us with behaviours where they did make a choice though – where they had the capacity to choose and made a choice that we feel is the wrong one, or that may be unsafe, or that breaks rules. They will test us and the limits we set to work out their place in the world. At these times, our children need consistent consequences. When we are consistent, we show our children that we are predictable, and in time they will adjust their behaviour. It is always the behaviour that we are addressing, never the child. The child is not wrong, the behaviour is. This is not about punishment, belittling or shame. It is about learning and growing.

Depending on the behaviour, there are different approaches that can be taken, all of which maintain the connection and support our child to learn. Here are a few options to use as appropriate:

- redirection
- natural and logical consequences
- loss of privilege
- time-in.

Redirection

When a child is engaged in behaviour that we want them to stop doing, a simple technique to get them to stop is to redirect them towards another behaviour that we are more comfortable with. It is not about just giving them a totally different thing to do, but instead about meeting the need that the original behaviour was supporting in another way and addressing the need verbally too.

For example, if your child is picking at the wallpaper and peeling it off the wall, there may be an underlying sensory need that this behaviour is meeting. Discuss this with them and find another activity that meets that need. Explain in a calm way why picking at the wallpaper is not an option. Try to do this in a curious and questioning way (although that can be challenging). Might picking labels off jars meet the same need? Or ripping up paper or boxes from the recycling? Explore alternatives with your child to find a solution that works.

Or what if your child is angry and hitting out at another child. What else could they do to express this anger? Could they stomp? Or bounce? Or pull at something with strong resistance? Make sure you empathize and work through the big emotion with them. Help them to see that it is okay to have these big feelings – we all do – but finding ways to manage them that do not hurt others or ourselves is important.

When we redirect, we acknowledge the need, explain why an alternative is required, validate the feelings involved and support our child to find other ways of expressing these big feelings.

Natural and logical consequences

Putting the connection first and supporting our children to deal with their underlying need does not mean that we ignore negative behaviours. Children need feedback to learn which behaviours are acceptable and which are not. A consequence is a result of an action or situation. Consequences can happen naturally or be engineered. Consequences can be positive or negative. A positive consequence, such as praise or a reward, encourages a repeat of the behaviour. Where possible, focus on reinforcing positive behaviour and letting natural consequences happen to help your child to learn.

Natural consequences occur without our intervention. Children learn by doing. For example, if a child stands in the rain, they get wet; if they do not put their coat on, they get cold; if they forget their snack, they feel hungry at break. Let your child learn from these natural consequences themselves and resist the temptation to add to the discomfort that they already feel by telling them off. Show empathy for the predicament they find themselves in by saying things like, 'It must have been tough being cold at cricket. It is good that you have warmed up now though.' Beware of the pull of ending with a comment such as, 'Maybe you will remember your coat next time' as this adds to the shame that they are already feeling. It might be better to say something like, 'What do you think you could do differently next time?' to encourage reflection. It can feel uncomfortable as a parent to let nature take its course in this way. We instinctively want to step in to help them, but although that helps them in the moment it does not support them to develop the life skills they need. Stepping back and letting them learn for themselves teaches them about cause and effect and instils a sense of responsibility.

There are some occasions where we can give natural consequences a helping hand; where we can intervene in a way that the child sees the cause and effect and takes responsibility. This is not about punishment but about a consequence to an action that is fitting to the action. For example, if a child spills something, ask them to wipe it up; if they do not take their PE kit out of their bag, do not wash it, so they miss PE or must wear a dirty kit. Apply the consequence in a neutral way without judgement or criticism and explain how the consequence relates to the action. It is about them taking responsibility for the consequences, not about blame or shame. When we do this, we encourage our children to think, and our actions feel fairer as they are linked to what they did.

Tips for putting consequences into action:

Stay calm: When we are calm it helps our child to be calm too.

Focus on the behaviour: Always address the behaviour, not the child. This consequence is because they broke the house rules, not because they are a naughty child. This keeps the connection as your child feels loved even though they know their behaviour was wrong.

Give a warning: Give your child a chance to change the behaviour. Make the warning clear and specific. 'If you tip your chair up one more time, we will put the steady feet back on.'

Follow through: Mean what you say and do what you say promptly. 'I already warned you about tipping your chair. Stand up now so we can put the steady feet on, so you do not hurt yourself.' When your child knows that you will consistently follow through, the behaviour is more likely to reduce.

Be consistent: Use the same consequence for the same behaviour. Be predictable so your child knows what to expect.

Be timely: Action the consequence as close to the behaviour as possible and do not make it take too long.

Children need predictable consequences for their actions. When we want them to do something differently it may take time and lots of repetition. However, if we remain consistent, things will change. Although natural consequences are useful a lot of the time, they are not always appropriate. If a child is too young to understand or is doing something that is risky to themselves or to others, then adults need to step in.

Loss of privilege

Loss of privilege is when we take away something that our child enjoys as a consequence for their behaviour. A privilege is a luxury, something your child wants but does not need. For example:

- a favourite toy or game
- pocket money
- an activity
- a bike
- an electronic device
- screen time
- time with friends
- an after-school activity
- a lift to a social activity.

Ideally, the privilege would relate to the behaviour, but it is not essential as this can often be difficult to achieve. Whether the loss of privilege is related or not, it is essential that the child understands why this has happened.

For example, a related loss of privilege would be if a child leaves their bike unlocked, they lose access to it for the rest of the day. An unrelated loss of privilege would be if a child hits a sibling and so misses a trip to the cinema.

Here are some tips for using loss of privilege:

Stay calm: When we are calm it helps our child to be calm too.

Focus on the behaviour: As mentioned in 'Natural and logical consequences', always address the behaviour, not the child. This consequence is because they broke the house rules, not because they are a naughty child. This keeps the connection as your child feels loved even though they know their behaviour was wrong.

Be proportionate: Make sure the loss of privilege is reasonable and proportionate. For example, in the example above the child lost access to their bike for the afternoon, not for a week.

Be specific: Ensure that your child is clear on why this is happening and how long the loss of privilege is for.

Give a warning: Give your child a chance to change the behaviour. Make the warning clear and specific. 'If you throw the remote again the TV will be switched off for ten minutes.' Where the behaviour changes, praise your child for making the change. However, if the behaviour is dangerous to your child or someone else, then you need to step in straight away to keep everyone safe.

Follow through: Mean what you say and do what you say promptly. If the behaviour repeats or doesn't stop then follow through with the consequence. 'I already warned you about throwing the remote. I am switching the TV off for ten minutes till half past three.' When your child knows that you will consistently follow through, the behaviour is more likely to reduce in severity and frequency.

Be consistent: Use the same consequence for the same behaviour. Be predictable so your child knows what to expect.

Be timely: Action the loss of privilege as close to the behaviour as possible and do not make it take too long.

Stick with it: Sometimes your child may say that they do not care about the loss of privilege. If they do, ignore it, and continue with your planned course of action.

Use loss of privilege sparingly as it can be construed by a child as punishment. It is the consequence of last resort. Negative consequences work best when they are a small part of a larger set of positive consequences which encourage good behaviour, like connection and praise.

Time-in not time-out

Time-outs and naughty steps are much-used punishment methods that are heavily represented on TV shows about parenting. The child is told to go somewhere (like a corner or a step) alone for a specified number of minutes. During this time, parents ignore the child and any crying or calls for attention. Consequences like these that involve punishment and shame for a child are undermining and create dysregulation and disconnection. They are unrelated to the behaviour, can be confusing for a child, involve isolation, foster resentment, and set up negative narratives about themselves in our children's heads.

A time-in is used in the same situations as a time-out, but a time-in focuses on the connection with the child and on regulation. Instead of sending the child away, when we use a time-in, we remove the child from the situation but remain with them until they are calm. If your child is dysregulated, initially just sit with them, or near them, and give them time to come down naturally. If they do not want you to be in the room with them, sit by the door, but make sure they know that you are there and they are safe. This might be all that is possible at this time and if so, that is enough, the connection has been made and the child feels supported.

Sometimes just being together and feeling the connection is enough, at other times a conversation may be appropriate once they are calm and able to reflect. As you talk together, make sure to empathize with their feelings and help them to process them and consider whether other courses of action may have been available to them. What could they have done instead?

When we use a time-in, our child believes that their feelings are heard and accepted. They get the time they need to process these big feelings in a safe and supported way. They don't feel isolated or shamed and the connection is strengthened.

Don't use a time-in if you are feeling overwhelmed yourself. In that case, you may need to take a break from each other until you feel calmer. You can't support your child to regulate themselves if you are dysregulated. Perhaps come back to talk about things later in the day or at bedtime when you are both more able to connect.

Asking questions that open dialogue

Whether we are using redirection, natural or logical consequences, loss of privilege or time-in, we want to have an open and curious dialogue with our child about what happened, what they are feeling and what could be done differently. It can be challenging to think of what to say in the moment, so here are a few questions to draw from which fit a variety of different situations that you can use to get started and help you come up with lots more of your own.

Starting the conversation:

- When you are ready to talk, I am ready to listen.
- I am here for you whenever you want to talk.
- I am here when you are ready to talk.
- Can we take a deep breath together and talk about things?
- You seem really upset, what is up?

Asking about what happened:

- What happened? And then what?
- What happened next?
- What happened just before...?
- Where did...come from?
- What is happening when...?
- And where were you...? And where was x...?
- How did that happen?

Avoid asking questions such as, 'What did you do?' or, 'Why?' as these can sound accusatory and generate shame for a child.

Asking about feelings:

- It is important to me to understand what it is like to be you and what you are feeling.
- How did you feel?
- It sounds as if you are saying... Is that right?
- What needs to happen for you to feel...?
- What was the sad bit there for you?
- If I were you, I might feel worried about this – how about you?
- I can imagine other people feeling pretty hurt about that. How does it feel?
- Are you feeling more angry or hurt or...?
- How does that affect you?
- Is there anything about this that you feel embarrassed or ashamed about?
- Do you know what makes you feel upset about this, or do you just feel upset?
- What is the worst thing about that?
- What else is hard about that situation?
- Do you feel more sad/hurt/angry/worried about that, or some other feeling?
- Why do you think that made you so sad/upset/worried?

Using different words to name the feeling can sometimes help a child to feel understood. Different words have different strengths of emotion and may resonate more in a particular situation. Here are a few options to use in place of the old favourites of angry, confused, afraid and sad (although these will work well too):

Alternatives for angry: Annoyed, fed up, irritated, mad, jumpy, resentful, furious, agitated, fuming, impatient.

Alternatives for confused: Uncertain, doubtful, lost, flustered, rattled, stumped, puzzled, mixed up, unsure.

Alternatives for sad: Upset, weepy, low, helpless, hurt, powerless, miserable, unhappy, lonely, left out, guilty, sorry, embarrassed, overwhelmed, ashamed.

Alternatives for afraid: Panicky, nervous, shocked, frightened, worried, scared, stressed, anxious, petrified, frozen, jumpy, shaky, or uneasy.

Do not be afraid to go into big negative emotions; it can feel as if we are making it worse for them by dwelling on upsetting things, but the opposite is true. Bringing them out into the light robs them of the power they have when they skulk about in the dark. A problem shared is a problem halved.

Show that you are listening with empathy:

- I'm listening.
- That sounds hard.
- That's rough.
- So, you're saying...
- It sounds as if...

Avoid saying things such as, 'I totally get it' or, 'It could be worse' or, 'It'll be fine' or, 'Don't be upset'. It can be tempting to say these things, as they feel as if we are helping them to feel better, but these phrases are dismissing the child's feelings.

Learning for the future:

- What could you/I/we do differently another time?
- What might you/I/we keep the same?
- What other way could you/I/we have handled it?
- If you were the other person, what would you do differently?
- What's another way to look at this?
- What were your options at that point?
- What would be one step forward at that point?
- Is there anything you could do to change that?
- If you had unlimited powers to go back and change things, what would you do?
- What would make this a little better?
- If you could change anything about..., what would you change?
- Has anything else helped in the past?

Handling difficult situations together:

- We can work on this together if you like?
- Would you like some help with this, or do you just want me to listen?
- What do you think you/we can do about this?
- I can help you with this if you want or need me to.
- What do you need to know from me so that you will feel safe to talk to me about it?
- What can I do to help?
- Is there anything I could change that would make things better for you?
- What needs to happen for...?
- What would you like to happen?
- If you had a magic wand, what would you wish for?
- What would happen if...?
- What do you think might happen when...?
- How could you/we figure that out?
- What is your plan?
- I wonder how...
- I wonder what would happen if...
- I wonder what would happen if we changed this...
- What do you think might happen next?
- What made you think of that?
- How could you...?
- What do you see?
- What should we put here?
- Can you think of other ways to...?
- Do you have any ideas?
- How did you come up with that solution?
- Tell me how...?
- Do you have any ideas for solutions?
- Are there any other ways we could...?
- I wonder if...might help. What do you think?
- Is there someone else you would like to talk to about this?

Avoid telling them what to do. Ask questions that help them to think for themselves. It is okay to make suggestions but ensure that they are deciding rather than being told.

Checking in that there isn't more they want to talk about:

- Is there more?
- Is there anything else?
- Is there anything we have missed?
- What else is going on for you?

Acknowledging that they have opened up to you:

- Thank you for sharing that.
- Thank you for your honesty.
- That must have been hard for you, I'm glad you felt able to share it.

Avoid asking questions like, 'Is that everything?' or, 'Is that all?' as these can make the child feel that the right answer is yes and prevent them sharing more.

Some children are more aware of their emotions and more able to talk about what has happened than others. Be aware of their needs and only do what works for them and what they are comfortable with. When they are talking, give them time to finish. It can be tempting to jump in and interrupt or second-guess, but when we give them space, we allow them to think for themselves. Give them plenty of thinking time too. Children can take six seconds or more to process information (which can feel like an interminable time to wait), but if you can, when they look as if they are thinking, sit quietly to let them work it out.

Keep your language simple and appropriate to their understanding. Connect emotionally with them with your eyes, touch and body language. Keep your questions to one at a time. When we stack lots of questions together it can be confusing for a child. It's okay to empathize by sharing times when we felt the same, but keep it short; it is about them not us. Remember that they will experience things in a different way, so do not assume they feel the way you did.

Follow rupture with repair

As parents, we have the weighty responsibility of teaching our children to understand right from wrong, to know what is good and what is bad and what it means to have respect for others. Limits are an important part of creating structure for our children, but they can create tension and disconnection. Managing this tightrope is challenging and there will inevitably be times where we misstep or when our child resists our well-meaning actions.

Sometimes, even with the best intentions, conflicts will flare up that are intense and emotionally charged. These are times when we and our children lose control and engage in screaming and name-calling. These conflicts are distressing for both parties and create disconnection, guilt and shame. We can end up feeling helpless and inadequate and our children can end up feeling criticized and humiliated.

When this does happen, forgive yourself. We all make mistakes. We all get it wrong. I sometimes get it wrong in a spectacular fashion. It is what we do next that makes the difference. Every disconnection makes a perfect opportunity for reconnection – a perfect opportunity to apologize and teach our children that it is okay to make mistakes. A healthy relationship is not defined by there never being difficulties, instead it is defined by how we overcome them through connection.

Ruptures happen in relationships when the two sides get stuck in their own interpretation of a situation and are unable to see the other person's point of view. Repairing the rupture takes reflection, acknowledgment, sharing and curiosity.

Reflect: Once you are both calm, talk to your child about the fact that you have been thinking about what happened. Reflect on what you have been thinking and feeling and encourage them to talk about their thoughts too.

Acknowledge: Acknowledge what your child may be feeling and experiencing. This is a key part of repairing as it shows that you are listening and understand the feeling behind the behaviour. Acknowledge what you were feeling and experiencing. Connect with each other's recollection to understand each other's feelings and internal experiences.

Share: Tell them what you would do differently next time. Explore what you wish you had done differently and what you will try to do in the future. Think together about what would be different if there was a rewind button you could press. Show your child that you want to work on your connection and that we all make mistakes. Encourage them to share too. Say things like, 'I wish I had asked a bit more about how you were feeling rather than getting angry. Could you tell me now so we can try again?'

Be curious: Connect with them by being curious about what was going on for them at the time. Wondering about their internal experience helps us to understand them and helps them to build emotional intelligence and self-regulation.

Ensure that you tell them you love them at the end of the discussion, reinforcing the bond and the feelings you have for them. Ruptures are opportunities to strengthen our relationships. They show our children that even though we may fall out, we come back together again, and they demonstrate that the relationship is strong enough to weather storms and that our love is unconditional.

Chapter 8

ENCOURAGING A GROWTH MINDSET

If we were describing a child, would we describe them as not having long trousers, as not having short sleeves, as not having glasses? Or would we say they are wearing shorts, a long-sleeved t-shirt and glasses? Knowing what the child isn't wearing doesn't tell us anything about the child. We couldn't picture them from the description.

It seems odd to describe clothes in this way, and it is. However, our children are described all the time like this. They are described using deficit-based language, describing what they don't have, what they can't do, what they find hard. The child gets lost in the negative. We and school can get stuck focusing on how to make things better, on scaffolding our child to cope with situations, focusing on the problem. It is important to do this, as creating a framework around our child so they can succeed is essential. However, when we focus on this to the exclusion of everything else, we miss all the wonderful things our children can do. When we focus on what they can't do it can make them feel demoralized and unwilling to try. Focusing on their strengths, interests and talents at the same time as scaffolding them gives them the best of both worlds.

Identifying strengths

Here are a few suggestions to get you started on your own child's strengths:

Character traits: Are they kind? Helpful? Patient? Responsible? Serious? Funny? Are they optimistic? Loyal? Loving? Are they cheeky? Energetic? Loyal?

Social skills: Are they friendly? Are they sympathetic to others' problems? Do they give others space? Do they listen? Do they share? Take turns? Do they cooperate with others? Can they accept differences in others?

Language skills: Are they good with words? Can they tell a story? Tell a joke?

Literacy skills: Are they good at reading? At writing or understanding?

Maths and logic skills: Are they good with numbers? Or puzzles? Can they work things out? Are they good with mechanical things? Construction?

Creativity: Do they love to draw? Sing? Dance? Play music? Are they imaginative? Do they create their own worlds or stories?

Physical skills: Are they good at ball games? At cycling? At climbing, running or jumping?

Noticing their strengths makes us their greatest fans and helps them to see themselves in a positive light too.

Changing words changes minds

Words aren't neutral. Many words have a hidden weight of judgement that comes with them. Two words or phrases can appear to have the same meaning, but the way the person they are aimed at hears them can be very different. For example, one of my friends is very fond of joking that other people are opinionated whereas she knows her own mind. Opinionated comes with baggage, with implied criticism, whereas knowing your own mind feels like a positive, it feels like a personality trait we would all want.

There are lots of words like this that can be used to describe our children. These are words with a hidden judgement, words that imply criticism, words that create negative labels that our children carry like millstones around their necks. These are words that judge, that focus on a problem and ignore the strengths hidden beneath.

Here are a few examples and some alternative ways to view things where instead of being problem-focused, we zoom in on the solution and the strengths our child is exhibiting:

- Bossy – a natural leader.
- Defiant – has self-belief and is determined and tenacious.
- Demanding – good communicator, clear on what they want.
- Dramatic – committed, passionate, expressive.
- Fearful – careful, detail-focused.
- Fussy – knows their own mind, is clear on their preferences.
- Hyperactive – energetic, enthusiastic, lively.
- Impulsive – spontaneous, free-spirited, flexible.
- Oppositional – clear on their priorities, ready to fight for what they believe.
- Rebellious – free-spirited, confident in finding their own answers, not easily swayed.
- Stubborn – persistent, committed, steadfast, determined.
- Talkative – good communicator, outgoing.
- Tattletale – respects rules, cares about fairness and justice.
- Unfocused – multitasks, wide-ranging interests.
- Attention-seeking – loves connection, very social, a born entertainer.

When we focus on seeing our child's strengths, we encourage them to see them too. We help them feel good about themselves and proud of who they are. For example, my son notices everything around him due to his hypervigilance. He is the designated 'chief spotter' in the family and the 'finder of lost things'. He is also incredible at finding his way around and is encouraged to be our 'direction finder general' at every possible opportunity. These give him a wonderfully positive sense of self, of being useful and valued within the family and we find missing objects quicker than we used to and get lost less frequently!

Building confidence

We are not born with the ability to understand the world and our place in it. Babies internalize other people's perception of them, and this becomes their image of themselves. When a baby doesn't get good enough care, they feel that they are unlovable. Trauma skews their self-esteem. If our children are going to build the self-belief and resilience that we want for them, then they need to develop an inner sense of who they are and a belief that they are intrinsically good and that they are loved.

As much as we would like to cover our children in a cape of self-belief, it does not work that way. The reason it is called self-confidence is because it comes from within. How confident a person feels is based on what they think about themselves, not on what others tell them to think. So, telling our child that they are the greatest does not build true confidence; in fact it could result in exactly the opposite, giving children a sense of expectation which they feel unable to meet. To build true confidence we need to teach our children how to meet challenges, overcome difficulties and build coping skills, one brick at a time.

The first thing that we need to do in building confidence in our children is to think about what we expect of them. Are we expecting too much? Or too little? Are we setting them up to feel they have failed? We want to encourage our children, to support them to succeed, to create the environment where they will thrive. Creating that environment is a balance between helping them to develop and reach their potential while not setting them up to fail or creating undue stress for them.

Every child is unique, no child will be exactly at the developmental norms for their age, and children who have had a difficult start in life may be quite far adrift from these milestones. Avoid comparisons with peers or siblings. Benchmark them against themselves. Like us, children vary from day to day too. What they can easily achieve one day might feel insurmountable the next. Vary what you expect based on how your child is at that moment, be led by them.

I love you because...

Confidence and self-esteem are built on liking yourself, on believing in yourself and feeling happy to be you. For children, their self-esteem comes from the knowledge that they are loved and that they belong.

Work with your child to create two lists, each giving the reasons why you love yourself and why you love each other. I love myself because... I love you because... Do not just focus on big important things, small things matter too. They do not all need to be serious either. Do some silly ones. Include some for your child that they sometimes do, but you want to see more of, plant a seed that they can do it. Most of all, make it fun, enjoy yourselves.

Here are a few examples to get you going:

- I love my sense of humour.
- I love my flexibility.

- I love how organized I am.
- I love that I am so focused when I want something.
- I love that I can laugh at myself.
- I love my tiny earlobes.
- I love that I do silly things

And:

- I love your laugh.
- I love the way you chew your pencil when you concentrate.
- I love how hard you work at school.
- I love your sparkly blue eyes.
- I love the way you get so immersed when you are reading a book.
- I love how you keep on trying till you succeed.
- I love how helpful you are.
- I love your imagination – it is magical!

There are lots of fun images online that you can paste into documents and most children nowadays are very adept at this. Maybe they could give you some tips?

Where possible, talk about as many examples of them doing the thing as possible. Reinforce that it is something that happens all the time, that they are like this a lot and therefore loved a lot. When we think of good things about ourselves, we build belief in our own inner goodness. Supporting our children in focusing on who they are and what we see in them will give them a positive sense of self that will stand them in good stead for the rest of their lives. Spending time with our children provides them with opportunities to learn and to be heard. Most of all, it provides time to connect. It is these connections that make children feel loved and that they belong. Build their core belief in themselves and the mental durability they need to weather the small stuff – and life's bigger challenges down the road.

So, for a short while, ignore the emails and text messages, leave the chores for another few minutes and give your children your focus. Spend those extra few moments with them. When you look back, you will not remember the tasks you did not finish, but you will be thankful for the memories.

Giving effective praise

When we are praised, we may feel proud, happy, confident and ready to try anything. Sometimes we may doubt the other person's motives or may feel a little awkward or shy, but generally praise done well is a positive experience. Criticism or correction, on the other hand, brings up quite different feelings. We may feel embarrassed, angry, stupid, demotivated, rejected, ashamed and ready to give up.

Done well, praise can work wonders with children. Compliments generate good feelings that the child enjoys and wants to replicate, so they will make more effort to remember what to do and try again another time. It is important to note that how we feel when we are praised or criticized is clouded by our life experience and our resulting internal beliefs about ourselves. Children who have experienced trauma may have internalized low self-esteem. They may feel that they are somehow to blame, or are unworthy, or unlovable. Praise may be difficult for them to hear because it doesn't match their internal sense of themselves, and they may reject it or believe that you do not really know them or that they do not deserve it.

It can feel awkward and difficult to say nice things to others, and some of us struggle to give and receive compliments and praise. Sometimes it feels easier to criticize, but the more we practise giving and receiving praise, the easier it becomes, and the rewards are huge for us and our children.

Children usually want to please their parents, so praise can be a powerful reward that can give a child a deep feeling that they are worthwhile, loved and a good person. Does it follow that all we need to do to help our children build a positive and realistic self-image is to praise them? Unfortunately, as with most parenting, it is not quite as straightforward as that. The problem is that praising can be tricky, and sometimes well-intentioned praise can have an adverse effect on your child.

For example, how would you feel if a friend commented on something you were wearing and said, 'You are always so glamorous', or if other parents asked you to buy the Christmas present for the class teacher because, 'You always choose something fantastic and original', or if you hurriedly pulled a presentation together based on some old slides and a colleague commented that you 'are very impressive and did an amazing job', or your child said, 'You are the best mum in the world'?

Praise can make us doubt the person praising (If they think that was a good presentation, they must have exceptionally low standards). It can make you immediately negate the praise (Glamorous! They should have seen me before I did my hair). Praise can make you feel pressurized and anxious (Now I need to find something to meet their expectations of the fantastic present they think I will choose). Praise can make you focus on your insecurities (Best mum? I don't think so, look at all the things I do wrong). For our children, there is the additional complexity of their negative sense of self, which can lead to doubt and disbelief when their internal view of themselves does not match the praise that they are being given. When we are praised, it can feel uncomfortable, many of us can feel awkward or embarrassed at first, although many of us feel the positive vibe straight away. Everyone needs praise and encouragement, even if they initially find it hard to accept.

If your child rejects praise, don't be put off, persevere. Don't go too far too soon, take it slowly, one small drop of praise at a time. Think of it as putting water on a dry sponge. If you turn the tap on too fast, the water will bounce off the sponge, but if you take it slowly one drip at a time, before long the sponge will be saturated with water. With praise, little and often works best.

Yes, there are pitfalls, but effective praise is powerful and can work wonders with children. When we praise them, it can look as if the sun just came out on their faces; they beam with pleasure and pride and the impact is magical. So, what do we need to do to praise effectively?

Praise the effort not the result: This focuses on what they can control, like how much time they spend on a project or their approach to something. This kind of praise is empowering; it is not about natural aptitude but about how hard they are trying. Praising the effort encourages a growth mindset: 'You worked really hard to put your jacket on' rather than, 'Well done you put your jacket on.' Or, 'I am so impressed with how hard you worked on your science project' rather than, 'You are so good at science.' Children who are praised for the effort tend to prefer tasks that are more challenging and they are more interested in learning things. When the focus is on the result, it reinforces to the child that what they produce may not be good enough, whereas focusing on the effort emphasizes that working towards a goal and doing your best is what matters.

Give praise as soon as possible: Children live very much in the moment, so the quicker you do it the more effective it is.

Be sincere: A common error is to overdo the praise so that it becomes inauthentic and puts pressure on the child to live up to an expectation; for example, 'You're the best dancer in the whole wide world.' Children know when you're not being genuine. It makes them wonder why you aren't telling the truth.

Be specific: Instead of 'Good job' say, 'Well done, you put all the toys in the toy box' or, 'You did a nice job waiting your turn to talk while I was on the phone.' This clearly tells them what they did well. It also reminds them of the behaviours you want to see. When doing this it doesn't need to be gushing, in fact it's better if it isn't; it's okay just to describe what they did.

Don't follow your praise with a negative: 'You did a great job of eating up your breakfast. I wish you would do that every day.' This hurts the child's feelings and negates any positive message.

Talking about how you feel about what they did makes it real to the child: 'It makes me happy when you help your brother.' 'I felt proud when you scored the goal.'

Praise their strategies: 'You found a really good way to do it.' 'What a creative way to do it.'

Compare them to themselves, not others: Praise them based on how well they are doing compared to themselves, not other people. It is not about coming first, or beating another person, it's about trying hard and doing better than they would have done if they had not worked at it. Praise based on out-performing someone else is fleeting and can be undermined when they inevitably face stiffer competition another time. 'I'm so proud of you for all the work you put into learning and practising saying the poem' is more empowering than, 'I'm so proud of you for coming first in the class.'

Focus on progress: This helps them see that their efforts are paying off, which is motivating. 'I can see how much you have been practising your putting. You have a much better control of the ball's speed than you did when I saw you playing a few weeks ago.'

Talk about how their actions affect others: Show them that they are a valued member of the family and that their help is appreciated. 'Thanks for helping Granny with her garden this afternoon. I really appreciated you lending a hand and Granny was so pleased with how tidy it all looked.'

Praise your child for their persistence: 'I can see you've been practising.' 'Your hard work has really paid off.' 'How did you learn to do that?'

Over the next few days, find opportunities to praise your child. As you do so, observe how your child reacts. Do you notice anything different?

Guidance through feedback

Praise is essential to focus on our child's assets and strengths, but as a parent sometimes we need to guide our children, to help them to make better choices next time. So, how do we achieve this without criticizing them or making them feel shame or judgement?

A simple way to overcome this is to distinguish between criticism and feedback. Criticism is making a negative comment about a person. It blames and is focused on the child, which generates anger, confrontation and shame. It does not encourage improvement.

On the other hand, feedback is giving information about how to improve. It shows respect, is behaviour-focused, encourages cooperation and sharing, gives the child a chance to listen and explains how to change.

When we give feedback without criticizing, we separate the behaviour that we see from the child as a person. Here are two examples of criticism versus feedback in practice:

Example 1

Criticism: 'Look what you have done. You are so clumsy; you are always dropping things. Can't you pay attention to what you are doing?

Feedback: 'Oh dear! Toast on the floor! Can you pick it up and put it in the food recycling and we can make another slice? Next time you could put it on a plate, so it is easier to carry.'

Example 2

Criticism: 'What are you two shouting about now? Can't you play nicely for five minutes? How many times do I need to tell you to share?'

Feedback: 'It is not okay to talk to each other like that. You need to agree to share and work together or take turns. Which will it be?'

Here are a few hints and tips on giving good feedback:

The problem is the behaviour not the child: Don't say the child is bad, say that you didn't like what they did and explain what a better choice would be.

Encourage problem-solving: Help your child to come to their own opinion on what they could have done differently. Encourage them to think what else could have happened. Did it go as they thought it would? If not, why not? If they were doing it again, what would they do the same next time and what would they do differently? Why?

Solicit your child's point of view: Do not assume that you know why they did something. Ask what was behind the choice they made before you make judgements based on your view of the world.

Use a feedback sandwich: Put a negative point sandwiched between two positives and frame the negative as something to improve. For example, 'You did a really good job with your teamwork in the first half. I noticed how well you watched what the others were doing and worked with them. We might want to do a bit of work on your passing; we can practise in the garden tonight to improve your accuracy. Overall, I saw lots of great passing and moving into free space, your focus on the ball was great and you were a key part in the play that led up to the winning goal. Well done, I am proud of you.'

Keep it specific to this moment: Stay in the 'here and now', do not bring up previous mistakes.

Notice the small things: Highlight even small things that your child does.

Each time our children are recognized for doing something well in an authentic way so that they can believe it, it has a positive impact their sense of themselves.

Don't label your child: Children get their sense of who they are from what others tell them. When a parent gives a child a label, it can come to define them. Nobody wants to go through life feeling clumsy, fussy or even having a supposedly positive label like sweet or no trouble.

Avoid global comments: It doesn't help to tell a child that they 'always do something' as this leads them to believe that they are irredeemably bad. Instead, be specific. So instead of saying, 'You've spilt your drink; you're always spilling things' say, 'Oops, you have spilt your drink. Can you get a cloth to wipe it up? Maybe use a smaller glass the next time to make it easier to handle.'

Describe what you see: Keep your language neutral. 'I see your school shoes on the floor in the hall. Can you put them away please?'

Pick your moment: Don't give negative feedback if you are cross. Take the time (even if it takes a while) to be in a calm frame of mind before starting a discussion. If your child does a poor job of washing the dishes, help him to learn how to do it rather than telling him off; for example, you could say, 'I know you worked hard at washing the dishes, and I appreciate that. But I noticed that there's some food stuck on some of the plates. I used to do that when I was your age, too. Can I show you the way I've learned to wash dishes?'

Changing how we do things can feel cumbersome at first, but like all things, with practice it becomes easier. Keep working at it, and in time you will not even notice you are doing it, although you will notice the positive impact it has on family life.

Enhancing mental flexibility

Life is full of unexpected changes to plans, and problems and challenges to overcome. For example, your child is going to visit a friend in the evening for a sleepover. The morning before, you get a call to say their friend is ill and it must be cancelled. This is understandably very disappointing for a child; however, a child with good flexibility of thought will be able to focus on when they can reschedule and what they might do instead. A child with more rigid thinking may get stuck in the loss, feeling unable to consider doing it another day or doing something else instead.

So, here are some ways we can encourage our children to build more flexible thinking:

Chunk things down: We can help our children to think more flexibly by working through tasks with them and helping them to break things down into more manageable chunks. When they can see a big task as a series of smaller chunks it seems much more manageable.

Focus on options: When they are working on a problem, or a puzzle or a game, it helps them to see that there are multiple ways to do things. For example, if you are doing a jigsaw together, talk about how you could put all the pieces out first, or you could separate the edges from the inside parts, or you could sort pieces into colours or even shapes. There are lots of ways to approach it, and some will be more successful than others, but all are available.

Consider 'what ifs': Talk about 'what if' scenarios when they are doing things. Think up strategies ahead of time that can be used. By learning how to be more adaptable and embracing change in the little things each day, the child will be better equipped to respond when faced with a larger challenge.

Encourage ingenuity: Play fun games with them to use everyday objects in different ways. Work your problem-solving muscles. Think about how many things you could do with a paper clip for example. Encourage mental agility. See who can find the wackiest or think of the most unusual thing! Use the paperclip to hold paper, as a hook, joined together to make a necklace, as a phone stand – the possibilities are endless, yet we rarely see a paperclip in these ways. How often is that true in our decisions in life too? How many options pass us by unnoticed? So how about thinking up alternatives to any challenge you or your child face? Experiment with different strategies. By practising doing this you will both learn to think flexibly, to see the choices and therefore increase your options and your resilience.

Narrate your thought process: When you are thinking through options, do it out loud. Or tell your children later about the different options that you considered and what your reasons were for choosing the one you did.

What will happen next? Pause the TV or stop in the middle of a story and get your child to guess what might happen next. Think about options, what different things could happen.

Use mind maps: For a big problem, use mind maps to brainstorm through options. Add everything you think of, even options that you would not choose. Help them to see that there are always choices.

Practise small changes: Expose them to small changes in their daily life. Only do this when they are in a calm and resourceful state in case it wobbles them. Perhaps come home a different way from school. Or sit in a different seat at the table. Or play a game another way such as going backwards round the board or going up snakes and down ladders.

Teach them how to think, not what to think: When kids come to parents to solve their problems, the natural response is to lecture or explain. A better strategy is to ask questions. When we bounce the problem back to the child with our questions, we help them think about the issue and find solutions. Work with them to produce a list of ideas and weigh the pros and cons of each one.

Bringing flexibility into their everyday life to helps them see that there are different approaches and different ways of doing things and they can identify that there are choices. Enable them to see that there are always choices, that there are always opportunities to branch out in new directions. Work with your child to develop the skills that they need in life. Giving them strategies helps them to deal with things for themselves and equips them to face things with confidence, secure in the knowledge that they have the skills to overcome any obstacle. When we encourage openness, flexibility and willingness to change, we create resilience in ourselves and in our children.

Embracing mistakes

Dealing with change or setbacks is part of life. Sometimes these will be small, and sometimes they will be large. We may see them coming, or they may come out of nowhere. The only certainty is that there will always be challenges for us to face in life. All children encounter challenges as they grow. They can feel under a lot of pressure to do well at school, to excel at extra-curricular activities and to fit in and make friends. It can be all too easy for children to slip into a pattern of comparing themselves unfavourably with their peers and thinking they are not good enough. For children who have experienced early life trauma, these stresses are compounded by their life experiences and the impact that this has on how they view the world and their place in it.

Fear of failure

Fear of failure can be paralyzing. At the extreme it can lead to a learned helplessness where children avoid multiple activities where they feel that they cannot succeed. In some cases, this can rule out large areas like all sports, writing and any physical activity. When children become paralyzed in this way it becomes self-fulfilling: they do not try, so reinforce their fear and belief that they will fail. As a result, avoiding failure becomes their singular motivation and goal in life.

Failure-avoiding: Children may avoid any task in which there is a risk of failing. It is not about succeeding, they just want to avoid failing. To avoid failure, they do things such as make excuses (the dog ate my homework), procrastinate, do not participate, or choose near-impossible tasks. They believe that if they extend a lot of effort but still fail, then this implies low ability and therefore low worth. But if they do not try, they perceive that they have not failed, so there is no immediate impact on their self-esteem.

Creating an excuse: Children can also avoid failure by failing in the activity, but then protecting themselves from the failure by having an excuse: 'I would have done well, but I just didn't feel like it' or, 'I would have done just fine, but the teacher was totally unfair.' They stick to the belief that it is never their fault so they cannot be held responsible.

Over-achieving: Children may avoid failure by succeeding – but only with herculean effort motivated solely by the fear that even one failure will confirm their greatest fear: that they are not perfect.

At the heart of fear of failure is the child's belief that if they fail, in any arena – academically, at sport, creatively or socially – then terrible things will happen. They fear disappointing us, being ostracized by their peer group, feeling embarrassed, ashamed or worthless. Embracing mistakes (your own included) helps promote a growth mindset and gives children the message that mistakes help them learn.

Next time your child lacks belief in themselves and fears failure, try getting them to see it slightly differently. If they say, 'I can't do it...' or, 'I'm bad at this...' or, 'This is too hard', try empathizing with them by using one of these options:

- Tell me what makes you feel that way.
- It sounds as if you are struggling. How can I help?
- Is that really what you think? Or are you tired? You could stop for a bit and have a drink and a snack, then come back to it?
- It does look hard. I find things like this hard sometimes. Let us look at it together. Two heads are better than one.
- Let us break it down into little chunks and do it one piece at a time.
- I am confused too. Why don't we put a note on it for the teacher to get her to explain it to both of us so we can work it out?

When we use empathy and work with our child to solve something, we encourage them to keep trying and we build resilience.

Redefining failure

As a word, failure has extremely negative connotations. What if instead of seeing failure, we could enable them to see feedback? Initially this might seem a little strange but if you take it on board, it can transform the way you and your children think. The way that we learn is by making mistakes. Every 'failure' is valuable information about what did not work, and you can learn from it. The faster you make mistakes, the quicker you learn!

This does not mean that we should actively encourage our children to make mistakes and behave recklessly, but if they do their best and it does not work out, it is not a failure, it just did not work. The way we learn is by trial and error. Only by trying can we learn what works, and so learn what actions we want to keep doing. It is by trying different ways to do something that we get the feedback to enable us to improve and achieve our goals.

Develop a positive approach to making mistakes and help your children to do the same. Foster an approach of thinking, 'How interesting, what can I learn from that?' Help your children to build a more balanced view and generate an attitude of curiosity instead of focusing on what went wrong.

Don't see it as **FAIL**ure, instead see it as a First Attempt In Learning.

There are many examples of famous people who personify learning from failure, who had to try, try and try again. They persevered, they learned lessons from previous attempts and in the end they succeeded. If these people had not kept on trying, the world would be a poorer place.

So here are a few famous 'failures':

- Walt Disney was fired by a newspaper editor because he 'lacked imagination and had no good ideas'.
- Thomas Edison's teachers told him he was 'too stupid to learn anything'.
- As a child, Albert Einstein had some difficulty communicating and learning in a traditional manner.
- After Harrison Ford's first small movie role, an executive took him into his office and told him he would never succeed in the movie business.
- A young Henry Ford ruined his reputation with a couple of failed automobile businesses.
- While developing his vacuum, Sir James Dyson went through 5126 failed prototypes and used up all his savings over 15 years.

These are fitting examples to talk through with your children. It helps to reframe the idea that to be a success you need to always succeed. That is patently not true.

Learn from mistakes

Facing things that you are fretting about head on can make you feel more in control and therefore more confident. It is all too easy to get lost in over-analyzing things and concentrating on the negative. The next technique is a terrific way to help your child challenge their thinking about things that they perceive as mistakes or failures and reframe them as opportunities to learn.

When your child talks about an occasion where they perceive things went wrong, and they are focused on the fact that they made a mistake, get them to make a list of five things that went well or that they feel that they managed okay on that occasion. Now list the thing that they feel went wrong. Ask them whether it will still matter in a month or a year from now. How important will it be to them by then? Will they even remember? What could they do differently, or work on for next time?

When your child starts to talk about mistakes or 'failure' from their past, challenge them to write down all the positive things that came out of it, including what they learned and how it changed their life for the better in the long run. Beforehand, think about some occasions from your past where you felt there were mistakes or failures which in the end turned out not to be. Then you can use your own examples to illustrate the point and really bring it alive for your child.

Work with your child to help them to redefine what success is. Praise the effort they put in, even though they may not reach their goal. If they did everything that they could to achieve it, then no one can ask more of them than that. At the end of the day, will children be disappointed in not having achieved their goal? Of course, but there will also be the satisfaction of having given their best effort. Every child is unique and different, and what one child finds easy, another may never achieve. If they can focus on how hard they try and the effort that they put in, they will be rewarded for their behaviour. They are being praised fairly for their effort. When we praise effort, children are encouraged to keep trying, to value their achievements and to persevere.

So, what about the old maxim that the world is a tough place, and we need to teach our children to deal with failure? It is true that the world is often not a supportive environment. It *can* be a tough place to be. Even more reason for us to nurture our children and give them an innate sense of themselves, a belief that if they try their absolute best, they have done well. That way we equip them to deal with the slings and arrows that the rest of the world will throw at them.

Confidence comes from competence

Self-confidence rises out of a sense of competence. In other words, our children develop confidence not because we tell them that they are great, but because of their own recognition of their achievements, big and small. Of course, it is good to hear encouraging words from Mum, Dad or carers, but when children achieve something, whether it is brushing their own teeth or riding a bike, they get a sense of themselves as able and capable and tap into that high-octane fuel of confidence.

Building self-confidence can begin early. When babies learn to turn the pages of a book or toddlers learn to walk, they are getting the idea that 'I can do it!' With each new skill and milestone, they develop increasing confidence. Our children may not have had these positive experiences as babies. The shame, guilt, and negative beliefs about themselves and their place in the world that are often the legacy of early trauma can diminish our children's sense of competency. They may withdraw from activities, avoid trying new things, be highly self-critical or hold themselves to impossibly exacting standards.

We can help our children by giving them lots of opportunities to practise and master their skills, letting them make mistakes and being there to boost their spirits so they keep trying. We can respond with interest and excitement when they show off a new skill, and reward them with praise for their efforts. Then, when other important challenges present themselves, they can approach them knowing that they have already been successful in other areas.

Encouraging healthy risk-taking

We do not want to wrap our kids up in cotton wool, but we want them to stay safe. With children who may struggle to understand consequences or have poor impulse control, this can be a bit of a juggling act. It is easy to keep saying 'be careful' but that does not help our children to learn to risk assess or work out how to overcome challenges.

How do we help them to foster awareness while still encouraging them to try out new things?

Here are a few options to try that are more specific than 'Be careful!':

- Do you see how shiny those rocks are? They look slippery.
- Which stones look wobbly, and which look safe to step on?

Would it help to try them out by touching them with your foot before you step on them?

- As you walk through the water, feel ahead with your foot. That way you can tell what you are about to step on, or if there is a deep bit.
- Before you wade into the water, might it be a good idea to take some of your clothes off in case you fall in? That way you have some dry things to put on later.
- Does the branch the swing is on look strong? Maybe give it a tug first to see how strong it is? What is your plan if it does break?
- What is your plan? How will you get across? Could you use anything to help?

Asking questions that prompt them to reflect helps our children to learn and develop strategies of their own for next time.

Facing challenges with confidence

When facing a challenge, it can be easy to feel overwhelmed at the thought of things going wrong. Our brains can become trapped in a cycle of imagining and rehearsing the worst until it is hard to imagine anything going right. So much of the stresses that we and our children experience are created in our own minds. We are victims of figments of our own imaginations. We imagine the worst and amplify our fears until we are paralyzed. Voicing our fears and insecurities and putting them to the test can prove to us that things are rarely as bad as we see them in our minds. We need to help our children to understand this and realize that even when things do go wrong, they have the skills and strategies available to cope.

When they are worrying about a future event and fretting about it round and round in their heads, challenge them with the following questions:

- What are you worried will happen?
- How likely is that to happen?
- What else might happen?
- What is the worst that will happen? What would that really mean?
- If the worst did happen, what could you do to cope?

- What is the best that could happen? How would that feel?
- What is the most likely outcome?

Help them to put their fears into perspective. Break the cycle. Worries are never so scary when you drag them out of the shadows into the light and see them for the miserable specimens they really are.

Teach your children the analogy that learning things is like climbing a mountain. To get to the top, sometimes you will be going up, sometimes going down, that is the nature of things. Sometimes you will think you are reaching the top only to find a hidden peak still to climb. But even when you are on a downward stretch, you are still getting nearer the summit and can look down to see how much further on you are now than where you were at the start.

— Chapter 9 —

FAMILY, FRIENDSHIPS AND FRICTION

Managing relationships with others is an important life skill for adults and children. The way we interact with them, and our interactions as a family, model how relationships work. Healthy social development does not require that a child has lots of friends. It is about quality rather than quantity. Some children are more reserved than others and it is vital that we take things at a pace that they find comfortable.

The way we are with our children teaches them the skills they will need to build and maintain friendships, reduce friction and handle conflicts when they arise. Our children will behave with others in the way they see us behaving within the family. They will imitate our interactions with our friends as they interact with their friends. Model positive social skills and praise your child when they interact with others in a positive way. Point out when they greet classmates in a friendly way or when they take turns or share. Reinforce the social behaviours you want to see more of.

Creating a positive family culture

Build a respectful and supportive attitude within your family. Encourage activities where you speak positively about each other. It is good to get some perspective from time to time and step back and remember what you mean to each other.

Our children model the things that we do, so we need to think about how we talk to them and how we behave because that is what they will model and how they will behave. We also need to keep the channels open – to help them to understand how to get through things that are happening. We want to encourage their independence, but we need to ensure that they will come to us with their problems and want our input. We need to teach them how to cope with things themselves by working with them, talking to them, asking questions and being open to the way they think they should do it. We can ask things such as, 'What if you...?' 'Is there another way you could have done that?' 'What do you think the other person was thinking?' Be curious and ask questions that encourage them to think for themselves and get to the answer. In this way, we support them in learning and empower them but are still there and part of the process. In time, they will make more and more choices for themselves based on the strategies that they learn.

Model complimenting your children to their faces and praise them to others when they are in earshot. Compliment little things as well as big ones. Model saying nice things about other family members and about people outside the family too.

Telling and showing your kids that you love and value them is important. When there is a lot of conflict, even if it does not look like it, they will remember. Show them that you are the consistent person in their relationships and will not let them down. Remember as you forgive your child, to forgive yourself too. Parenting is tough and emotionally charged. We and our children are works in progress. We all have much to learn. I know I do.

Developing responsibility

If we want our children to develop a sense of responsibility, then we need to give them things to be responsible for – to include them in decision making, encourage them to stop complaining and start finding solutions. If we expect our children to be able to sort out their own problems, then we need to help them to see how differences can be settled without resorting to insults or physical means.

Having a family meeting where everyone has their say generates a sense of fairness and inclusion in family life and provides a blueprint for children to use when dealing with choices or problems in the future. It encourages a sense of responsibility and maturity in our children if they are involved in decision making.

The meeting could be about a specific topic (where to go on holiday, whether to get a pet, who does what chores in the house) or more generally about family life, looking at what you could do more of, do less of, stop doing, start doing. A family meeting is a very constructive way of including children in decision making, offering them a framework to raise their point of view and hear others' perspectives in a calm and controlled setting.

The idea of having a family meeting is not to hand over the reins to the children, but to give them some say in the decisions that affect them. This helps them to feel empowered and listened to and develops vital life skills because as they grow up children will be expected to make larger and larger decisions about their lives.

Encouraging curiosity about others

Children learn about the world by taking in what they see around them and creating their own model of the world from that. They make assumptions that what is around them is how the world is, and how it should be, because it is all they have known. They stereotype the world based on physical traits like race, gender and age. They categorize the world and are likely to identify with people who are similar in appearance to themselves. When they see things that are different from the worldview they have created, it can feel scary and confusing.

Help your children to see that the world is full of difference, and to embrace those differences. Talk about how it is okay to like different things and about how that is what makes us individuals. Talk about how boring the world would be if everyone were the same. Talk openly within your family about diverse cultures, races and religions. Talk about different types of relationships, about disabilities that can be seen and those that are hidden. Be inclusive in your language and encourage your child to be open and accepting of difference. The more our comfortable our children are with diversity, the more they will accept the differences in others and the stronger their relationships will be with everyone.

Instilling a focus on finding solutions

Adults and children alike are very keen to point out what is wrong – to criticize how things are done or what others are doing. This is not constructive and fosters conflict. What if, instead of complaining, we encourage our children (and ourselves) to focus on what the solution could be? What if we ask questions that prompt reflection and move their thoughts away from complaining about the past to constructive reflection on how to change things for the future? These could be questions about what could be different and what would be better. They could be questions that are curious about what might be going on for the other person; questions about what the constraints may have been to make things that way; questions that focus on practical solutions and empower our child to become the driver of their bus instead of a passenger, and teach excellent problem-solving and negotiating skills.

Breaking the cycle, not the connection

Society pressures us to believe that there are lots of things we must and should do as parents. There are rules and ways of behaving that our children must adhere to and that we as parents must ensure that they do. This results in multiple negative interactions and puts a lot of pressure on us and our children. When we succumb to this pressure, our interactions with our children get filled with instructions, filled with us constantly picking at our children's behaviour and nagging them to do things which still do not get done. We get cross, they get cross, and things escalate and descend into conflict.

When we are in conflict with our children, we are breaking the connection. Reducing the conflict is about choosing our battles; it's about prioritizing stability and calm, stepping back and thinking about what matters and what is important to us.

What is more important – that our child holds their fork properly or hangs their coat up? Or that we sustain our connection with them?

When we step back, we gain clarity that the most important thing is the relationship we have with our children. The connection that we have with our children is built from shared experience, from the moments where we laugh, cry, talk or are just together. The intimacy comes from all these tiny moments. Building this deep connection with our children is founded on making that attachment our priority.

What if we did not deal with everything at once? What if we prioritized what we focus on with our children? This does not mean that we never focus on the behaviours, just that we do things a few at a time and as we accomplish our main priorities, other things move up into the top slots. When we prioritize and only focus on a few things, it takes the pressure off us and off our children.

Start by thinking about all the things that cause conflict with your child: list them all, big and small. Be specific. Here is an example list to help you start to think:

- talking over the TV
- shoving things down the side of their bed
- holding cutlery correctly
- not eating with hands
- keeping mouth closed when eating
- brushing teeth
- not hitting siblings
- running in the supermarket car park
- doing piano practice
- how much time they spend on their laptop/ipad
- what they wear
- time watching TV
- crossing the road safely
- eating all their food
- putting things away
- leaving things all over the floor in their bedroom
- saying please and thank you
- throwing balls in the house
- leaving toys all over the garden
- washing hands and face.

Once you have your list, decide which are the most important. Which involve safety and must be tackled first? Which are big flashpoints for your family? Which would make the biggest difference in everyday life? Put these as your top priority for immediate action. Only have a maximum of five that you focus on.

Here is an example of the top five priorities for focus for one child:

- hitting siblings
- running in the supermarket car park
- shouting at siblings
- crossing the road safely
- brushing teeth.

These immediate action behaviours are where you put all your energy and focus. Leave the rest for now. When they happen, let them go. By ignoring the less urgent things, you take the pressure of your child, and you may find that things calm down and some of the lower priority things on your list, which were fuelled by anxiety, will reduce naturally. The more we work on reducing the points of conflict, the more we build the connection with our child because when the conflict is less, it frees more space in our day to have positive interactions.

As time goes on and things change, revisit your list and decide what your new top priorities are.

Facilitating repair

Although we can reduce conflict, it is not realistic or healthy to expect that relationships will be harmonious all the time. People are not perfect, and relationships are messy, so resolving conflicts is part of life. Within families, there will inevitably be arguments, there will be tension and hurt feelings, and there will be disconnections.

Conflicts will arise because sometimes we will be busy, preoccupied or grumpy and will miss the cues our children give us. These times are inevitable – we are human and are often pulled in many directions at once. Where we set boundaries, there will be inevitable disagreement. In these moments, we and our children can become disconnected and conflicts can flare up. Sometimes these conflicts will become heated and things will be said that will be regretted on both sides.

We will all lose our tempers with our children. I do it all the time. It is not about being perfect, about never getting angry, but about what happens next. The repair. Saying sorry, admitting that we are wrong, seeking their forgiveness and showing that we made a mistake is a crucial step. It rebuilds the relationship where the shouting and anger has broken it. It repairs the ruptures that result from these mis-communications and gives our children a model of how to apologize. It shows that it is okay to be wrong and that it is strong to apologize and to own up to your mistakes.

When we are in conflict with our children, nothing positive will come from trying to resolve things while everyone is still cross. No one can think rationally and behave with reason when their emotions are heated. Take a breather from each other. Make space for you both to calm down and be able to talk.

Once you are both feeling more able to talk calmly, have a conversation about what happened and what the problem was. Talk in a place where you both feel comfortable, and you are at their level. Sitting alongside each other can be good as it takes the pressure off. Take your time, do not rush – this is a great opportunity for you to connect with them and to show them how a conflict can be resolved successfully.

Identify and acknowledge the hurt your words and actions have caused. Whether this was intentional or not, if the other person's feelings were hurt, we need to take responsibility. Check in with the other person to check that you understand how it felt for them.

Listen actively and state the reason for the disagreement, using their words before you respond to it. For example: 'I get that you were disappointed earlier and would rather have gone out with your friends than been at Granny's. It is tough to feel left out.'

Define what happened using 'I' messages and focus on feelings so that any judgement, accusation and blame are removed. For example: 'I was hurt by what you said.' Ensure that you apologize, and ideally include regret, responsibility, remedy and repair. 'I am sorry I shouted. I know I should have been calmer and that it scares you when I yell at you. How about we sit down together and watch a film and we can arrange to have your friends round tomorrow?'

Saying sorry (and meaning it) is sometimes all that is needed to repair the connection. Do it unconditionally without blaming the child, justifying your actions, or glossing over what happened. Do not go overboard either. Be calm and concise. Apologizing can be tricky for adults. How we were parented might lead us to believe that adults do not need to apologize, that we are in charge.

When dealing with your child, be fair, be consistent, put in boundaries and stick to them. If we are inconsistent, then they will not feel secure. Make any consequences relate to the behaviour. For example, if they threw a friend's toy and broke it, they must give them one of their toys to make up for it.

The art of negotiation

When things get heated, we can end up entrenched in our own position, convinced we are right and determined to win at any cost. At this point, a peaceful resolution can feel out of reach. Practising negotiating skills within the family defuses conflict, creates respect for each other, and builds connection. Negotiation involves empathy and compromise. When we as parents teach our children to negotiate with us, they will also negotiate with other adults and with their peers and in the process enhance their confidence and social skills.

Have a few ground rules to ensure that things are as calm as possible:

- When you approach the other person, be open and prepared to listen.
- Define the problem up front. Make sure everyone is clear on what the argument is about.
- Do not interrupt. One person talks at a time. If this proves difficult, you can have a physical object that the person who is talking has in front of them to highlight that they are the speaker, and no one talks while they are talking.
- Keep it in the here and now. Keep old, unrelated issues out of it.
- Understand each other's point of view. Put yourself in their shoes. Ask questions if you need to be clear on what they think. Look for their good intention.
- Encourage everyone to leave blame out of it. Keep the person out of it. Use 'I feel...' statements.
- Encourage active listening by reflecting the other person's point of view.
- Remember that the end goal of the conversation is not for someone to be proved right or to win. The end goal you are all aiming for is a mutually agreed solution. Highlight that both sides will need to be flexible, and that compromise will be needed to reach an amicable solution.
- If yelling starts, the discussion needs to stop. Get everyone to step back and walk away. You can try again once everyone is calm and ready to talk.

Children feel empowered, respected and independent when we encourage them to negotiate and take control of their choices. If we embrace negotiation, compromise within our family, and encourage our children to share their opinions, feelings and needs, we teach them to take ownership and honour and respect others in the same way. Negotiating with our children is not giving up or giving in, it is teaching them an important life lesson.

Reducing conflict between siblings

The relationships between siblings can get fractious. We can end up feeling more like a referee than a parent, running about blowing our whistle and issuing frequent red and yellow cards. Dealing with squabbles between siblings can feel relentless and emotionally and physically draining.

Conflicts are inevitable, but we can reduce the frequency and intensity and help our kids to build more rewarding relationships with each other. Creating a respectful culture within the family will have a positive effect on the way siblings interact.

Treating your children fairly rather than equally is essential to creating an environment where everyone's needs are met. Celebrate their individuality, do the things with each child that they love to do. They will have different interests and may require different things depending on their age or stage. One child may need more scaffolding or have fewer demands than the other. Ensure that support is given in an open way so that neither feels hard done by.

When conflict does arise between siblings, do not get dragged into the turmoil. Stay calm and use measured language. Do not get involved in blaming or comparisons to each other, or to previous occasions. Ensure that each can express their point of view and listen carefully, acknowledging their feelings. This ensures that they feel heard, but it does not mean accepting negative or aggressive behaviour. Talk to them about what happened, encourage them to verbalize and reflect on what went on and why. Brainstorm some strategies for handling things differently another time. If necessary, talk to each child separately to avoid blaming and shaming. Our aim is to support our children to learn and to rebuild their relationship, not to correct or punish.

Nurturing friendships

Friendships are the training ground where children learn how to have a good relationship with others and develop strategies to avoid conflict or deal with it when it is unavoidable. They learn to cooperate, to share and take turns. They learn about other people's feelings, about differences between individuals; they learn to manage disagreements and to repair broken relationships. Childhood can be a tough time. Teaching our children practical skills to nurture their friendships in a healthy way, to communicate their needs and wants, to negotiate, empathize and cooperate, will help build strong and lasting friendships and enable them to navigate everything from small squabbles to major breaches in their relationships.

What makes a good friend?

We can support our children to learn about what being a good friend means in day-to-day family life; for example, when they are playing with a friend or sibling and are deciding what to play or who gets a particular toy. When these situations crop up, we can support them by narrating what is going on, explaining what is happening and why. Do this for when they get it right as well as when they are struggling. Help them to think through their choices and learn for future times.

For example, we might say, 'I heard how you took turns and listened to each other before you decided what to play. That was a great idea and it helped you to choose something you both wanted. It feels nice when we cooperate and listen, doesn't it?' Or if they are not reaching an agreement, say, 'It is tough to choose sometimes, isn't it? What if we made up a story together where you both got a turn with the toy?'

Model talking and listening. Chat about different things, take an interest when they are talking about something they are keen on. Ask questions, encourage communication and cooperation. Model winning and losing too. When you play sports together, or board games or card games, show them how to win or lose graciously. Enable them to practise being elated or disappointed in a safe family space.

We can sometimes get stuck in a pattern of only talking to our children about friendships when things go wrong. Chat about friendships at other times too. Ask questions about what makes a good friend, about their friendships and what they mean to them. Help them to explore the relationships they have with others, to learn and apply that learning to their social skills as they move through life. Here are a few questions to help you think about things to ask them from time to time as you chat:

- What makes you want to be friends with someone?
- What makes it easy or hard to talk to someone?
- What is important to you about your friendships?
- When your friend is sad, cross or disappointed, what could you do to help them feel better?
- How can we disagree with someone in a nice way?
- Why do you think misunderstandings sometimes happen with friends?
- What does it mean to cooperate?
- What are some ways you can be a better friend?

Exploring what makes a good friend helps our child understand what they value in their friends and how to behave in ways that make them a better friend. It also helps them see when someone is not being their friend so they can act appropriately.

Learning about friendships

Friendships give our children a sense of belonging, build self-esteem and develop social skills. Some children find making and maintaining friendships easier than others, but every child will need help from the adults around them in negotiating relationships. Look for opportunities in everyday life to talk about friendship. Use real experiences that happen to them or to you; talk about books, films and TV programmes. There are examples of good and bad interactions all around us and these offer a great resource to initiate conversations with our children about friendships and how relationships operate.

Support your child to develop empathy by reflecting on how their actions impact on others. Ask questions such as these:

- How does it feel when someone gets cross with you?
- How does it feel when someone is nice to you?
- How does it feel when someone shares and takes turns with you?
- How does it feel when someone includes you in their game?
- Why is it a good idea to think before you act?
- How does it feel when someone tells tales about you?
- How does it feel when someone talks about you behind your back?
- How does it feel when someone boasts about something?
- How does it feel when someone bosses you around?

Talking with your child about how they felt when someone else did these things to them helps them understand the impact on others when they do these things. It helps them to learn from their experiences and apply that learning to how they interact with others.

Making good choices

Children can sometimes try to control others, which can create conflict and damage relationships. They may also feel angry about, or responsible for, things that are out of their control. Each day, every child will be faced with many situations where they may struggle to self-regulate and control big emotions that come up. They may face negative emotions like disappointment, anxiety, anger, loneliness and jealousy, and positive ones too, like excitement, happiness and hilarity. All these big emotions can make a child feel dysregulated. When they feel like this, they can make poor choices which can impact on their relationships. When children struggle with understanding what is in their control and what is not, they can sometimes seek to control things that they have no control over, which can lead to conflict with others. Understanding the difference between what they can and cannot control allows them to act on the things they can control while encouraging them to let go of the things that they cannot.

Teaching our children to understand what is in their control helps them to see that they have choices, that there are many things they do have a say in as well as those they do not. Understanding this helps them to build relationships and avoid or manage conflicts. This is a tricky concept to get across, but creating a visual representation of it can make it much clearer.

The comparisons of what we can and cannot control can be simply represented by two circles.

With anything new, children need to be familiar and comfortable with it before they apply it for real. An effective way to introduce the concept is to think about some general examples first and whether they are within or outside their control. Here are a few generic examples to get the conversation started:

- the weather
- how tall they are
- what they say
- what someone else says
- what day it is
- when they get up
- how hard they try
- whether they do their homework
- how their brother/sister acts
- when it is a school holiday
- what happens in another country
- whether their team wins or loses.

Add some personal examples that are particular to your family: things like mum dancing in public, the dog snoring, dad being grumpy – things that mean something to them and add a bit of fun.

Once they have the idea, you can draw your own circles of control like the ones above, adding things that resonate with your child. Keep a copy where they can see it, and add to it as new things come up.

When a problem arises, prompt your child to consider, 'Is this inside or outside my control?' and to think about where this sits on the circles. Over time, they may be able to add things to the inner circle as they become more able to control different things. The circles become a visual manifestation of their progress.

Standing up for yourself

Children need to learn how to stand up for themselves, how to get their point across and how to say no in a way that respects others and does not create conflict. We want our children to be able to build and maintain positive relationships that meet their needs and the needs of others.

When we communicate a need, we can do it either passively, assertively or aggressively.

Passive: When we are passive, our thoughts are not voiced and our needs are not met. Other people may take advantage of us and push us around. We may hide our feelings and not speak up for ourselves, avoiding confrontation at all costs. When we are passive, we can disappear into the background and others do not notice us or listen to or respect our opinion.

Aggressive: When we interact in an aggressive way, the other person feels bullied and put down. They may feel scared or threatened or retaliate with anger and aggression themselves. Aggressive communication can involve shouting, interrupting, or talking over others, making demands without listening. It can involve using insults and defamatory language to diminish the other person and treating interaction and differences of opinion as a power struggle, often using confrontational body language. It can lead to hurt feelings and may damage relationships as the other person does not feel heard or respected.

Assertive: When we interact in an assertive way, the other person feels respected and able to see our point of view. Assertive interactions are clear and constructive and strengthen relationships because our own needs and the other person's needs are both listened to and respected. When our children see us behaving in an assertive way, communicating our needs and opinions calmly and clearly, they learn that it is okay to stick up for their own needs and to put forward their views, and that this can be done in a way that is neutral and amicable and not at the expense of another person.

Model being assertive and using compromise and negotiation by speaking up when you need to, by using a calm and confident voice to state your needs and by letting your child see you saying no and showing that you mean it with them and with others.

Dealing with conflicts with friends

When our child has an argument with a friend it can be hard not to intervene to try and fix things for them – after all, it is hard to see them upset. And sometimes when we see our child in pain, we get angry at the other child and it is hard not to take sides. As we are emotionally involved it is natural that we have strong feelings. The experiences our child is having could also trigger memories from our childhood, amplifying our reaction.

However, if we intervene or control our child's friendships, we are not helping them develop positive relationships in the present or the future. As with many aspects of parenting, the best thing we can do is to equip them with tools to use that will help them with the immediate problem and stand them in good stead for life. We must encourage them to think for themselves and do their own problem-solving.

Conflicts cannot be resolved in the heat of the moment. If you are present when the conflict occurs, make sure everyone has cooled off before any dialogue to resolve things takes place. If you are hearing about it after the event, discuss with your child what they could have done to cool off in the moment.

Help them to think about what other options might have been available to them. Talk through options with your child. Help them to know that there are choices and that it is possible to avoid conflict or to stop it from getting worse. Talk through different options that they could think about the next time a possible conflict arises or they feel they are getting angry. Such options include going to play with someone else, counting to ten, walking away to cool off, taking turns and sharing, asking them to stop, or saying sorry. Give your child tools to think about how strong the emotions are, perhaps a score out of ten or a red, amber, green scale, and help them to decide their next step based on that.

Use 'I' messages to state feelings. Part of what makes conflict so challenging is that it brings up big feelings. Encourage your child to tackle the feelings first. For example, 'I feel hurt when you say that to me' rather than, 'You hurt me'. Encourage them not to do any name calling, blaming or interrupting. When we use 'I' messages we take responsibility for our own feelings whereas 'you' messages blame and lead to the other person becoming defensive and closing doors to communication. The 'I' messages defuse things and lead towards resolution rather than escalation.

When we support our children to interact in an assertive way, we ensure that they speak up for their own feelings while still respecting the feelings of others. Support your child to see that their perspective is not the only one. The other child has a view too. Work with them to consider what the other person may have been thinking or feeling; what may have led to them saying and doing the things they did. Foster empathy. Help your child to see that there is always another side.

In most conflicts, both parties have some degree of responsibility. However, most of us tend to blame rather than look at our own role in the escalation. When we take responsibility, we shift the conflict into an entirely different gear, one where resolution is possible. Help your child to work out what the source of the problem is. For example, if they are arguing over a toy, it might be about the fact that earlier one of them was playing with a new friend and the other's feelings are hurt. The anger is not about the toy but about something else entirely. Getting to the root of the problem helps them to understand and resolve it.

Look for a compromise solution and ensure that all parties are involved. Resolving conflicts is a creative act. There are many solutions to a single problem. The key is flexibility and a willingness to seek compromises. Empower your children to find their own answers. It can be tempting tell them what to do, but something they think up and agree upon on their own will be more successful. Help them to evaluate different solutions by asking if a particular option will make them feel better. Or will it make them feel worse? Or the same? Encourage your child to listen carefully to the other person and to speak honestly and kindly.

A handshake, hug or kind word gives closure to the resolution of conflicts. Forgiveness is the highest form of closure. Writing it down before they say it can be helpful and sometimes this can lead to a letter which they could give to the other child with whom they are in conflict. Encourage them to include the words 'I am sorry' and to say what they are sorry for. They could also add how they will fix it and not do it another time.

Encourage your children to accept someone apologizing to them graciously; to say thank you and acknowledge the effort that the other person went to and that it may have been hard for them. This helps to mend the relationship and strengthen the connection.

The next time a conflict arises either between yourself and your child, or between your child and another person, work through these steps to talk it through to resolution. Afterwards, think about how it went. How did it feel? What was better? What can you learn for the future?

Children's friendships change and alter over time. Some fallings out are temporary, others more long lasting. Let your child know that being friends does not mean that they will always agree or get along all the time. Support them to work out how they can make up with their friend again (if that is what they want). Listen to them and help them to identify and understand their emotions so that they can move on past the immediate anger and hurt. Once they feel able to, help them to brainstorm some options to move things forward. Support them to develop tools to deal with conflict and resolve it, being respectful of their needs and the needs of the other person. Encourage them to be assertive and seek solutions in a cooperative way.

Friendship difficulties can happen for many reasons. It can be because your child is shy or lacks confidence or they may like to take control. It may be that the dynamic in a friendship group has changed, and they or another child are being pushed out. It may be that another child is being aggressive or bullying. The playground can be a challenging place. The good news is that you can help. Talk to them about what makes a good friend, practise skills like listening, sharing and negotiating. Discuss examples that happen in real life, in books and on screen. Help your child to know what makes a good friend and what will make them feel less worried about their friendships.

Supporting your child to make new friends

If your child struggles with an initial approach, give them some conversations starters. Simple things like, 'Hello I'm...', would you like to play with me?' or, 'I like your shoes' or, 'Do you have any pets?' will get the ball rolling and initiate a conversation. Having a prop like a toy or game can help too.

Help your child to recognize when someone is having a tough time. Show them how to do things that reach out to the other person with kindness. Try simple things like sending a card or a text, making them fairy cakes or a friendship bracelet – anything that shows the other person that they are thinking about them.

Welcome your child's friends to your home. For playdates for young children or where the children are building a new relationship, some forward planning will help things to go more smoothly. Have some activities on hand such as crafts, baking or games. You will need to stay with them initially, but as things become more natural you can step away and leave them to it.

Where your child has friends who move away or go to another school, support them to keep the friendship going, and if they remain close geographically, encourage it yourself by organizing playdates. These out-of-school friendships are a wonderful way for your child to interact with others outside their immediate school peer group and can be invaluable when school friendships go through a rough patch as they provide a separate avenue for socializing.

Encourage activities that relate to their interests: sports, dance, crafts – anything that they enjoy and where they are likely to meet others who share their passion. Increase their chances of meeting new friends and maintaining those friendships. Taking part in after-school clubs and extra-curricular activities is a wonderful way to build new friendships. When doing activities outside the school day, make sure that your child has the headspace left to participate. If their bucket is already overflowing at the end of a school day, adding additional things in may be too much and they may be better going home to recharge their batteries.

Childhood friendships go through many ups and downs. If things are tough for your child now, try not to be too worried. Making friends and being a good friend are skills that can be learned and improved, so focus on helping them develop their friendship skills. The more opportunities we give our children to use their social skills, the more adept they will become. In time, things will fall into place.

— Chapter 10 —

TAKING CARE OF YOURSELF

Parenting children who find regulation difficult can lead to us becoming unregulated too. We can end up being pulled into their drama and chaos and before we know it, we are all spiralling down together. When our children constantly need us to be emotionally there for them, we have insufficient recovery time. If we do not have time out for ourselves, or someone to share our experiences with, we can become burned out. Being empathetic to them leaves us vulnerable to internalizing some of their pain. We may discover unresolved trauma within ourselves triggered by our children's experiences. Our children's hypervigilance creates hypervigilance in us as we seek to identify and mitigate any possible triggers for them.

We love our children with all our hearts, even when they reject us. Their emotional need can sometimes be greater than one human can provide. Despite this, we keep on trying to pour love into our children, hoping in our hearts that love will be enough even though our heads know it will take more than that alone.

Looking after children who have had early life trauma is challenging for everyone involved. Parents turn to professionals for support with challenging behaviours; however, the professionals may not have the background in working with traumatized children or may not have the relevant experience or training. This can lead to them reaching for answers that have their roots in more traditional methods, which can leave us feeling lost and isolated when we most need help.

Our children can present very differently to the outside world than they do at home. Our children can appear calm at school but explode like a shaken cola bottle as soon as they get home. Sometimes professionals do not believe our accounts or blame our parenting for the difference. They may see the explosion at home as evidence of a problem at home rather than as evidence of a something generated at school which the child can only release at home once they are in a safe space.

Sometimes we feel we cannot be honest about our children's behaviours. It can feel disloyal, and we do not want the world to judge our child who has already suffered so much. Often, people outside a family are only seeing the tip of the iceberg; they are only seeing a tiny amount of what the parents live with and are immersed in every day. Well-meaning friends and professionals can seek to empathize with phrases such as, 'All children can struggle with that' and, 'All siblings argue'. This is not helpful and in fact can seek to increase feelings of isolation. Children who have suffered trauma are not the same, they need different responses to thrive. It is like telling someone who is blind that we understand their life experience because we sometimes close our eyes. It is not the same and starkly highlights the lack of knowledge and understanding we have to face on a regular basis.

We can feel isolated because of things our child may be doing. They may not be extremely negative behaviours; it can just be that we are having to put so much in that we end up running on empty. We can feel exhausted by constantly second-guessing what we and our children are doing. This can lead to a downward spiral where we feel as if nothing works and nothing changes. I know there have been times when I have felt helpless, hopeless and depressed; times when I have felt alone, judged and blamed; times when I have felt useless as a parent and burned out with nothing left to give.

Burnout is a state of physical and emotional exhaustion. It is quite common in parents when we are dealing with long-term stresses. We worry that we will not get everything done, we worry for our children. We lurch from crisis to crisis feeling extremely far from the parents we thought we would be, feeling we have failed, feeling guilty, and all this worry means our sleep patterns are disturbed so we feel more anxious and irritable, and the cycle feeds itself.

Common signs of burnout are:

- feeling overwhelmed
- lacking energy or feeling exhaustion
- feeling helpless or trapped
- feeling isolated
- being defensive and sensitive to rejection

- feeling irritable and prone to anger
- having a negative or cynical view on the world
- feeling shut down and distant from emotion in others
- feeling that you are failing or unable to cope
- procrastinating and taking longer to get things done.

When this goes on for a prolonged period, we can move into blocked care where we distance ourselves from our children in an act of self-protection. This happens instinctively to shield ourselves from our child's dysregulation and challenging behaviours. In blocked care, we can shift to a kind of autopilot, meeting our child's basic needs while being unable to meet their higher emotional needs. We become reactive, dealing with problems, trapped in a negative cycle. We feel guilty, as if we are failing and do not get any of the positive interactions that would give us a sense of fulfilment as parents. We can feel as if we love our children but do not want to be with them as it is just too overwhelming.

When things feel overwhelming, remember to take:

- one thought at a time
- one task at a time
- one day at a time.

If you feel you are in burnout or blocked care, try to avoid guilt and blame. Recognize that you are finding things difficult and that it is understandable. You are dealing with a lot and are doing the best you can at this moment. Feeling overwhelmed and seeking help is not weakness. Remember that we are more than one thing at once. We can be resilient and still need a break. We can be independent while reaching out for help. We can love our child and still struggle with their behaviour; we can want to be parents while feeling burned out. Give yourself permission to have bad days, or bad weeks, to make mistakes, to ask for help, to feel all the complex and often conflicting emotions that you are feeling. It is okay to be imperfect, to be undecided and unsure of your next steps. Feel compassion towards yourself and think about the progress you have made. Know that you are not alone. There is no magic wand to make burnout and blocked care disappear; however, noticing the signs is the first step towards changing things, and there are some key areas to focus on that can make a difference, which we will look at in more detail in the following sections.

The first step in helping your family starts with you. No matter how much you love your children and want to take care of them, you still need time for yourself. It might seem selfish to spend time on yourself when your children need so much from you. But if you are going to be able to help and support others, you need to find time for yourself. In life, as on an aeroplane, you need to put your own oxygen mask on first before you assist others.

If we want our child to value themselves, we must show them that we value ourselves. So, take some time for yourself, build your resilience, and help yourself to help your child. It is not selfish to want your child to have a calmer, happier parent. Give your child a gift. Take better care of you.

Take a moment for you

When we get stressed, there are lots of small things we can do to help ourselves feel better, such as getting out in nature for a walk, creating a to-do list to get the thoughts out of our heads and onto paper, being creative. Do something that shifts gear and enables you to regroup. Sometimes it is as simple as sitting down and having a cup of tea and reading a magazine; something small and manageable. Doing something that we want to do as opposed to something we have to do makes all the difference. Building self-care into our day can operate as a breaker to stop the stress building up. Managing our stress enables us to parent our children better.

Taking time for ourselves does not have to be something that we have to plan for or that takes up a lot of time. It can be as little as a quick check in with how you are feeling, and take under a minute.

Time to stop

When we are rushing back and forth meeting everybody else's needs, we lose sight of ourselves. Checking in with ourselves gives us a chance to think about what our priorities are. Think about how you are feeling right now at this moment.

Stop. Take a moment, put both feet on the ground and wriggle your toes to feel the contact with the floor.

Take a big breath. Feel your lungs fill with air, breathe out long and slow.

Observe what you are feeling, your emotions, the physical sensations in your body. What are you thinking?

Proceed with the one thing that is most important right now. Take your focus to moving forward one step at a time.

Stopping for a moment to prioritize our next step gives us a chance to regroup and be ready to move forward.

Change your focus

It can be easy to get stuck in a spiral of negative thoughts inside our head. Particular times of the day can be extremely stressful, and we can fall into thought patterns that are making things worse and building our stress. Mealtimes can be an incredibly stressful period in many families. I know that was true for us. When we are in these situations, we can get stuck repeating the same thoughts day after day – thoughts about our children's table manners, about their squabbling, about how we feel they should behave, about how we wish things were; thoughts about ourselves and our ability to cope. These spiralling thoughts pull us down, we feed our irritability, our sense of hopelessness, and end up angry and overwhelmed. If you feel yourself falling into a negative thought spiral, try one of these techniques to break the cycle:

5,4,3,2,1: Look around you and list five things you can see, four things you can feel, three things you can hear, two things you can smell and one thing you can taste.

Count something: Count the flowers in the garden, the books on the bookcase, the peas on your plate. Use anything that is around you that you can focus on to redirect your mind.

Pick a colour: Look for things around you that are a particular colour. As you do, notice how drawing this colour to your attention makes you more aware of how much of it there is around us. Taking our focus away from our inner world into the outer world that surrounds us helps us to break the thought cycle we are stuck in and reset.

Do something backwards: Recite the alphabet backwards, or your address, letter by letter – anything that occupies your thoughts.

Play a song in your head: Sing a song in your head or recite the lyrics. Bring your focus to something that you enjoy.

Let it all go over your head: Imagine you are sitting on a rock at the bottom of the sea. Down here it is calm, all the waves and currents are far above you. Look at the fish swimming by, the fronds of seaweed drifting, and feel the water support you. Look up and see the waves far above. No matter what is going on up there, it remains calm down here.

Giving our mind something else to focus on distracts our thoughts and halts the spiral. It gives our nervous system a moment of calm to regroup.

Take a mental holiday

When we think about things that are upsetting, our body tenses up. This is because the lower centres of our brain, which regulate body functions, do not distinguish between real images and those which are imagined. If you think about being in an uncomfortable situation, your body will begin to respond as if you are in that situation. Since you have probably had lots of experience thinking about things that cause tension, you have all the skills necessary to do just the opposite. Instead of imagining something that makes you feel uncomfortable, imagine something that makes you feel good.

To prepare for your mental holiday, relax your muscles and take a few deep breaths. Then close your eyes and imagine you are in a place you enjoy. It could be the beach or the mountains, a favourite childhood spot, or a quiet woodland glade or somewhere you enjoy doing a favourite activity. Fully experience this imagined event. See the sights. Hear the sounds. Feel the air around you, the temperature, the emotions. Smell the smells. Tune in to the sense of well-being.

Close your eyes and let your worries drift away. Imagine your restful place. Picture it as vividly as you can – everything you can see, hear, smell and feel. Visualization works best if you incorporate as many sensory details as possible, using at least three of your senses. When visualizing, choose imagery that appeals to you; do not select images because someone else suggests them or because you think they should be appealing. Let your own images come up and work for you.

Enjoy the feeling of deep relaxation that envelopes you as you slowly explore your restful place. When you are ready, gently open your eyes and come back to the present. Now you have your happy place with you always, stored safely in your mind, and whenever you want to you can go there and be at peace again.

Massage away your tension

Self-massage can be a great stress buster and tension reliever. It only takes a minute, and the benefits are immediate.

To relieve tired eyes: Close your eyes. Place your thumbs under your eyebrows, starting at the inside corner of each eye socket. Press and gently move the thumbs in tiny circles, working slowly towards the outsides of your eyebrows and continuing this movement all around your eyes, ending back at the bridge of your nose. Repeat this several times, spending a little extra time at the indentation of the inner eye socket, where the bridge of the nose meets the ridge of the eyebrows – an especially tender point on many people.

To ease headaches and tension: Start by placing your thumbs on your cheekbones close to your ears and use your fingertips to gently apply pressure and rub the temples. Using very firm pressure and a tiny circular motion, gradually move your fingers up along your hairline until they meet in the middle of your forehead, massaging your entire forehead and scalp as you inch along.

To relieve neck tension: While sitting at a table or desk, pinch your hands over your shoulders. Breathe out, letting your head drop back as you slowly squeeze and pinch moving across your shoulders towards your neck. Then rest your elbows on your table, allowing your head to drop forward slightly. Massage your neck from your shoulders to the base of your skull using your fingertips to make small deep circles in the muscles on either side of your spine. Place both hands on the back of your head, interlacing the fingers. Drop your head forward and let the weight of your elbows pull your head gently down and feel the stretch in the muscles of your neck.

Easing those aching muscles makes us feel better physically and mentally too. Placing our focus on our body for these few moments helps calm the mind.

Identify your priorities

Each one of us has an internal set of guiding principles that define who we are. These core values drive our behaviour and inform our choices in life. When what we do matches our values, we feel satisfied and contented. But when our lives and actions do not align with our values then things can feel wrong, and this can lead to a deep feeling of unease and unhappiness. Making a conscious effort to identify our values helps us to bring more of what nourishes us into our lives.

What you value

When we define our values, we discover what is truly important to us, what feeds our soul. It is hard to do this in the abstract, so a good place to start is by identifying times when we felt good, felt confident, felt balanced and comfortable in our own skin. The following questions will help you to identify these times. Ideally think of a few examples of each to give you lots of occasions to reflect on, but if you are struggling to find examples then that is fine too. Do what feels right for you.

Think about times when you felt happy: What were you doing? Were you alone or with others? Where were you? Is there anything that springs out about this experience that contributed to your happiness? When you look at the list of values below do any of them feel as if they were underlying your happiness?

Think about times when you felt proud: What were you proud of? Was it a personal achievement or something someone else did? Which of the values on the following page link to this feeling of pride?

Think about times when you felt fulfilled: What were you doing? Where were you? Who were you with? What was it that led to the feeling of fulfilment? What values below were being met on that occasion?

Think about times when you felt contented and at peace: Where were you? Were you inside or outside? What about the experience generated the feeling of peace and contentment? Was it the setting? Was it what you were doing? Or who you were with? Which values from this list resonate with this feeling?

You may want to choose values that are not on the list, and that is fine – it is about what resonates with you. These are your values, no one else's.

Accountability, Accuracy, Achievement, Activism, Adventurousness, Altruism, Ambition, Authenticity, Balance, Being the best, Being a good sport, Belonging, Boldness, Calmness, Carefulness, Caring, Challenge, Cheerfulness, Collaboration, Commitment, Community, Compassion, Competitiveness, Connection, Consistency, Contentment, Continuous improvement, Contribution, Control, Cooperation, Courage, Courtesy, Creativity, Curiosity, Decisiveness, Dependability, Determination, Diligence, Discipline, Discretion, Diversity, Dynamism, Effectiveness, Efficiency, Empathy, Enjoyment, Enthusiasm, Equality, Excellence, Excitement, Expertise, Exploration, Expressiveness, Fairness, Faith, Family, Fidelity, Financial security, Fitness, Focus, Forgiveness, Freedom, Fun, Generosity, Goodness, Grace, Growth, Happiness, Hard work, Health, Honesty, Honour, Humility, Humour, Inclusion, Independence, Ingenuity, Inner harmony, Inquisitiveness, Insightfulness, Integrity, Intelligence, Intuition, Joy, Justice, Leadership, Legacy, Love, Loyalty, Making a difference, Mastery, Merit, Obedience, Openness, Order, Originality, Perfection, Positivity, Practicality, Preparedness, Professionalism, Prudence, Purposefulness, Reliability, Resourcefulness, Restraint, Rigour, Security, Self-control, Selflessness, Self-reliance, Self-respect, Sensitivity, Serenity, Service, Shrewdness, Simplicity, Speed, Spontaneity, Stability, Strength, Structure, Success, Support, Teamwork, Temperance, Thankfulness, Thoroughness, Thoughtfulness, Timeliness, Tolerance, Tradition, Trustworthiness, Truth-seeking, Understanding, Uniqueness, Unity, Usefulness, Vision, Vitality, Vulnerability, Wellbeing, Wisdom.

Once you have your list of values that made each of the experiences above memorable, look to see if any of them combine into one key value. For example, if you have included belonging, connection, family, and community in your list of values, you might say that connection is one of your top values.

Once you have your condensed list, prioritize them into your top five. There are two options to do this. Either give each of the values in your list a mark out of ten to order them and choose the five highest scorers, or prioritize them by comparing the first with the second and asking yourself, 'If I could satisfy one of these, which would it be?' Then compare the loser of that first comparison with the next one on the list and so on until you get to your top five. Either way, you will end up with a list of your personal core values.

Making congruent choices

In our lives, we are aware of making thousands of choices – big choices like whether to change jobs, move house, buy a car, and little choices such as what to wear, what to make for tea, which TV programme to watch. We are aware of making many of these choices every day but there are many other choices happening every moment that we are unaware of. These are choices that are made automatically without our conscious awareness; choices about what we take in from the world around us, what we choose to notice; choices about how we interpret that information and how we react; subconscious choices where we follow a path well-travelled, acting on autopilot.

Making choices that are congruent with our values does not have to be about making substantial changes. Small shifts in focus and behaviour can make big differences to feeling better in ourselves and about our lives.

For example, when I worked on my own values, I identified that one of my key values was feeling connected. I realized that I often felt disconnected from others, from friends and family. I identified a few small steps I could take to feel more connected. Meeting a friend for a coffee, reaching out on Facebook, messaging friends, saying yes to social activities rather than avoiding them because I was too tired, doing small activities with my children at home. Understanding how much I valued being connected helped me to see how important it was to my health and well-being to prioritize this. It helped me to seek out more of what met my need to be connected.

At the same time, I focused on the interactions I had with others and noticed what I was thinking. I noticed the times when my mind focused on the disconnection, where it focused on feeling as if I did not belong, where narratives ran in my head about the differences in my life to the lives of the others I was with. When I noticed I was thinking in a way that highlighted the lack of connection, in a way that made me feel that my value was not being met, I challenged the thought. I looked for connection, for similarities instead of differences.

These next two paragraphs will help you explore what you value and get more of that in your life too.

Taking intentional actions that fulfil your values: Your list of values and the situations that you identified where you felt happy, proud, fulfilled and so on will give great insights into activities, people and settings that meet your values. What things could you bring into your life now that would mirror these times? It does not have to be an identical experience – if one of your examples was that you felt calmness on holiday on a Caribbean island it does not mean you have to go jetting off on holiday. It's more about breaking that down into the constituent parts to bring more of that into your daily life. Could you get a sense of this by visiting a local beach? Or by interacting with nature? Or by doing a meditation around being at the beach? Or just by having a notebook with a picture on it that brings that feeling? Is there a smell that brings it to life for you? Or a sound? Or what if one of your values is creativity and you felt this doing art at school? What ways can you meet that need in daily life? Doing crafts? Making things? Decorating? Upcycling? Building things with the kids? The more we intentionally bring things into our lives that meet our values, the better we feel about ourselves and the more able we are to cope with challenges.

Noticing when your values are being met: We only notice a fraction of what is going on around us. Our brain is constantly filtering the information that we take on board. Our brain works like an algorithm on Facebook, showing us more of what we paid attention to in the past and hiding things we have not historically paid attention to. This reinforces a belief by showing multiple things to support it and nothing that negates it. When we become stuck in negative patterns of thought, our brain will only show us what it thinks we are interested in. Often these negative cycles are highlighting areas in our life where we are not meeting our values. In my personal example above, I realized I was automatically noticing where connection was not happening, reinforcing my feeling of disconnection and making me feel unhappy and unfulfilled. If you notice that you are doing this, challenge the thought. Ask yourself, is this true?

Is this how someone else would interpret this? What if I believed the opposite? What can I notice here that meets my value?

Perhaps do a dry run to get the hang of it. Think of a time in the past when you felt your values were not being met and challenge that perception to see it another way. Doing this takes time and lots of repetition, but it will change how you view the world and help you to see that your life matches your values in many more ways than you previously noticed.

Values exist, whether we acknowledge them or not. Our lives can be easier when we honour our values and nurture our inner needs. Our values are usually constant as they are linked to our core beliefs about ourselves. However, as our lives change, our personal values may change too. Staying connected with what we value is worth revisiting periodically, especially if we start to feel unbalanced and do not know why.

Nurture yourself

When we are busy looking after our family, we prioritize their needs and forget ours. Ironically, the more we neglect ourselves, the less able we are to care for them. If we are constantly running on empty, we become irritable and impatient, we distance ourselves from others and skip things we and our children love through exhaustion and overwhelm.

There is a difference between self-soothing and self-care. Self-soothing is an immediate reaction to stress. As adults, we soothe ourselves with food, with alcohol. We distract ourselves on our phones, we play computer games or watch rubbish on TV. There is nothing wrong with these behaviours – sometimes they are just the right thing to help us decompress. However, although they may give us a short-term respite, they do not address the underlying problem.

Self-care is about nurturing yourself, about being compassionate to yourself, accepting yourself and meeting your own needs. It is not about changing who you are or pushing pain or bad feelings away. Is not about doing what other people say you should or about becoming a better person. It is all about you – about what makes you feel good.

How full is your bucket?

Just like our children, we have a finite capacity, a limit to what we can take before we overflow into burnout. What do you have in your bucket for today? What could you take out to give yourself a bit of headroom?

At the start of the day, think about how you are feeling. Are you already tired and jaded? Is your bucket already half full or more? Where that line is indicates what capacity you have available today. Sometimes it will be more, sometimes less. If your bucket is already feeling quite full, consider what you can put off for today. Is there anything that can wait? Is there anything you can ditch completely or postpone? Aim to add as little to the bucket as possible on days when you have limited capacity remaining. What could you do to reduce the level of your bucket? Some things that you enjoy or help you feel more content? Or maybe today you just need to rest, have some down time. If you do need a day off, reframe doing nothing. Think of it as resting, or recovery, or a mental health day or a parental time-out. Give yourself permission to take what you need to regroup ready to fight another day.

Five-minute stress busters

Sometimes when our mind gets stuck in a loop, we need to do something short and sharp to change things up, to break the cycle and reset our thoughts.

Zoomies: Put on your favourite track and go up and down stairs quickly to the verse, and do star jumps to the chorus. These few minutes of vigorous exercise will release a burst of endorphins to calm you down and make you feel energized.

Don't just think it – ink it: Expressing our feelings could be the best way to deal with stress. Keeping a journal is a way to capture those feelings at any moment. You do not have to worry about what others think or say, this is your private journal so just let your pen do the work. By the time you are done, those feelings will be on their way out of your system.

Call a friend: We all have someone whose voice alone cheers us up. Give them a call, even for a few minutes. Whether with a joke or a funny story, or just by listening, they will most likely put a smile on your face and calm you down.

Sing your favourite song loudly: You might feel ridiculous at first, but you will also feel happier before the last verse is done. Just go for it, throw caution (and your dignity) to the wind, take a deep breath and let rip.

Wiggle it: Moving your toes (and your fingers) helps you stretch your body and gets your blood pumping again. The secret is that the wiggle does not usually stop at your toes but will probably lead to a full-on stretch, which rejuvenates your body and mind. Take off your shoes to really give yourself room to stretch and wiggle.

Breathe to calm the mind and body

There are lots of signs that we are becoming stressed. I start compulsively tidying to impose order. I feel my mind overthinking things, thoughts racing round, and I become short tempered, frantic and snappy.

When we feel stressed, we tend to take rapid, shallow breaths from high up in the chest. Over time this can become ingrained and lead to feelings of tension in the body and it can fuel feelings of anxiety. Breathing exercises are a way to manage anxious feelings, so breathe into the depth of your lungs, slow your heart rate and feel calmer.

If something happens, or your child does something that triggers you into an emotional response, take a moment to process what is happening. Stop and breathe, tell yourself it is going to be okay. If you need to, walk away, or have a glass of water. Focus completely on yourself and your reaction as you breathe. Learning to sit with an uncomfortable emotion is not easy; however, fully feeling the emotion means that we release it. If we try to supress or distract it, we make it stronger and more likely to return.

Surfing the wave of emotion

Emotions come like a wave, they rise, reach a peak and fade. If we notice them and accept them, they will pass in a couple of minutes. Think about where the emotion is in your body; is it in your neck, your shoulders, your throat, your chest or stomach? Really notice it and, as you do, breathe into it. Focus purely on the physical feeling, let go of your thoughts and focus fully on how it feels in your body. Accept the feeling, do not judge yourself, it is okay to have this feeling. Accept that this is 'just how it is'. As you breathe into it, the feeling may grow or it may lessen, it may move around your body or feel different. Remember that the feeling will come, and it will go. It will not last forever; it will pass. Notice as the feeling begins to fade, as you feel more peaceful. Notice as it falls away, like a wave breaking on the shore, as you continue to breathe into it.

By focusing in on yourself rather than reacting outwards, you are learning how to regulate yourself and making new pathways in your brain. Each time you do this the pathways will get stronger and stronger until they become your automatic response to a stressful trigger.

Breathe in calmness

When we are tense, our breathing becomes shallow and rapid. If fact, most of us do not breathe properly, whether we are tense or not. For these breathing exercises, all you need is a pair of lungs, your breath and a few minutes. There is no need for any other equipment, and they can be done wherever you are: while cooking dinner, in the playground, at the traffic lights, in the middle of a chaotic morning – any time, any place. Use these to keep calm and carry on:

Equal breathing: Inhale through the nose for a slow count of four, then exhale through the nose for a slow count of four. As you become more adept you can increase the count to six and then eight.

Abdominal breathing: With one hand on the chest and the other on your tummy, take a deep breath in through the nose, ensuring that the diaphragm (not the chest) inflates with enough air to create a stretch in the lungs. The goal is six to ten slow, deep breaths per minute for ten minutes each day to experience immediate reductions to heart rate and blood pressure.

Alternate nostril breathing: Hold the right thumb over the right nostril and inhale deeply through the left nostril. At the peak of inhalation, close off the left nostril with the ring finger, then exhale through the right nostril. Continue the pattern, inhaling through the right nostril, closing it off with the right thumb and exhaling through the left nostril.

Notice the positive

As we have already seen, we all filter the world based on our own life experience. When we feel low, our minds bring us more things to match that feeling. We filter out the positive and let in the negative. As this happens automatically, we are not aware of it occurring. We accept it as fact when actually it is our selective perception. We see the world in a way that fits with our mood or what we believe to be true. It is the opposite of wearing rose-tinted glasses. It is more like wearing dark blinkers. When we take them off, everything looks brighter. The outside world has not changed, it just looks that way. When we are focused on the negative things about ourselves, about others, about the situations we are in, we dismiss or forget everything else. We can learn to notice the positive as well as the negatives, even when things are tough. To do this takes a bit of effort at first. It took a while for these filters to build up so it will take a bit of repetition to change them.

Break the worry cycle

When we are stressed, our filters focus on the negative and discard everything else. When our reality seems negative, we can slip into a pattern of worry where we see the worst in everything. A pattern where we project ahead, feel that we are all doomed and see disaster around every corner. As Shakespeare said, 'Cowards die many times before their deaths; The valiant never taste of death but once' (Julius Caesar, Act II, Scene 2). Now that is not to say that fearing for our future makes us all cowards – far from it – but it does highlight how when we are anxious, we can create a sense of the world as a fearful place and a sense of the future that is very pessimistic.

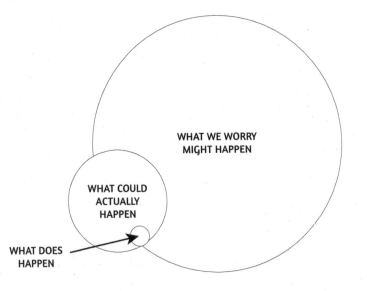

Worrying about all the things that might happen fills our mind and overwhelms us. Of all the thousands of things that we worry about, only a small number are possible, and only a tiny fraction of those will happen. And there are other possibilities that we never even consider that could and do happen. All that worrying is not productive; it cannot stop bad things happening and can lead to a spiral of worrying. Worrying about things that might happen stops us enjoying life in the present.

When you catch yourself stuck in worrying thoughts, challenge them with these questions:

- What is the evidence for and against this?
- What is the effect of thinking this way?
- Is there another more realistic way to see it?
- Am I coming to this conclusion without all the facts?
- What would a friend think?
- What if I look at the situation positively? What changes?
- Will I still be worrying about this a year from now? Five years from now?

Find your tribe

Human beings have a fundamental need to belong, to feel part of something, to connect with others and to feel that we are understood. When we feel stressed and overwhelmed, we often distance ourselves from others or, when we do interact, we find these occasions disappointing when those we are interacting with us just don't 'get it'.

In anthropology, the term tribe is used to define a small group of people who share a common bond. Each of us will have multiple tribes with whom we will connect. Reach out to groups online that represent interests you enjoy. Find parent groups that will be able to relate to you and your family. Look into training courses in things that interest you. Many of these can now be accessed remotely, which can be helpful if getting out is a problem due to childcare. Volunteer to do things locally; you can do some of these with your child and they are a wonderful way to connect with like-minded people. See yourself as the multifaceted person you are, open yourself to opportunities and see where they lead you.

— Chapter 11 —

A FINAL THOUGHT

We all live busy lives and have so much to juggle that we can lose sight of what we want, who we are and what is important to us. We may not have had optimal parenting ourselves and our children can push these buttons. Sometimes we can find ourselves struggling to keep our heads above water and deal with everything that is happening. The needs of our children take over, we put all our effort into keeping them afloat and our own needs get washed away.

Parents everywhere worry about doing things wrong. We feel that we ought to be able to handle parenting better than we do. We end up feeling disappointed in ourselves and certain that everyone else is coping better than we are. The reality is that every parent will feel this from time to time. We all want the best for our children, and we all worry that we are not doing a good enough job.

If you took on a new career or hobby, you would not expect to be an immediate expert. You would realize that there would be a learning curve, that you would find some things easier than others and that it would take time for you to learn. Why should parenting be any different? Why do we assume we should automatically be experts?

Parenting is a work in progress. We are all learners. Parenting has evolved through the generations and for each of us it is our own personal journey of discovery. We do not need to be perfect; it is good to be human and for our children to see that in us. A loving relationship is not one in which hurt never happens, or where mistakes are never made. The most fulfilling relationship with your child is possible when it is regularly renewed through shared experience, through acceptance and understanding of each other, flaws and all.

As a parent, I have made many mistakes. I have been impatient, irritated, pushy, controlling and there has been a lot of shouting! That is okay.

None of us is perfect. Being a good parent is not about being perfect, it is not about never making a mistake. Good parenting is about having a willingness to acknowledge our errors and lapses openly, to be humble enough to apologize when necessary and to accept ourselves as the work in progress that we are.

Look back at where you were and how you thought parenting would be before you became a parent. You have done more and meant more to your child than you could ever imagine. Think about how far you have come on your parenting journey to be the parent you are today. We all have shortcomings, we all make mistakes, but even if you feel you can make some improvements, you have come a long way already. The secret to contentment in life is accepting the situation as it is rather than how you think it should be.

Look forward – think of all the times ahead and how you already have so much wisdom to use for the future.

Go forward into the future with confidence. Take credit for all the amazing things that you already do, and all the amazing things that you will do in the future.

You've got this!